William George Etler Cunnyngham, Collins Denny

**A young People's History of the Chinese**

William George Etler Cunnyngham, Collins Denny

**A young People's History of the Chinese**

ISBN/EAN: 9783337166748

Printed in Europe, USA, Canada, Australia, Japan

Cover: Foto ©ninafisch / pixelio.de

More available books at **www.hansebooks.com**

A MANDARIN OF THE SECOND CLASS.

# A YOUNG PEOPLE'S

# HISTORY OF THE CHINESE.

BY W. G. E. CUNNYNGHAM, D.D.,
*Nine Years a Missionary in China.*

WITH AN INTRODUCTION BY
REV. COLLINS DENNY, M.A.,
*Vanderbilt University.*

FLEMING H. REVELL COMPANY:
CHICAGO; NEW YORK; TORONTO.
PUBLISHERS OF EVANGELICAL LITERATURE.

# TO MY GRANDCHILDREN.

# PREFACE.

The object of this small volume is to furnish our young people some general information about China and the Chinese. In a catalogue of two hundred and fifty books on China, now before me, I find but three intended specially for the young, and these are small biographies, containing little besides personal incidents. To add something, however little, toward supplying this deficiency in our juvenile literature, the following pages have been prepared. A consecutive history of the Chinese, running through the long and dreary centuries of their existence, was of course impracticable. To dwell upon their peculiarities only, might amuse but would not greatly profit the youthful reader. I have therefore endeavored to select such salient features in their national character and history as would enable a person of average intelligence to form some just idea of the country and the people. How far I have succeeded in this attempt, the reader will judge.

Previous to the beginning of the present century, comparatively little was known in Europe or America concerning the people of China or their institutions. Enterprising travelers, from the days of Marco Polo, had now and then touched at points on the coast of China, and reported, with more or less accuracy, what they had seen; but until 1842 no foreigner was allowed to travel or reside on the sacred soil of the "Celestial Empire." So that China was, to the people of the West, practically an unknown land.

At the close of the "opium war" with England, in 1842, five ports on the coast of China were opened to foreign commerce, where foreign merchants were permitted to reside and conduct business with the natives. Christian missionaries were also granted the privilege to live and labor at the open ports; but the interior of the country was still closed against all "foreign barbarians." Under these annoying restrictions missionaries and merchants remained in China until 1858, when, by the terms of the Tien-Tsin treaty, their privileges were greatly enlarged. Four new ports were opened to trade; the navigation of the great river, the Yang-tse, was made free to all nations; foreigners were allowed to travel through the country; Christianity was tolerated, and missionaries given liberty to reside anywhere in the empire. Such is the condition of affairs in China to-day, and such the privileges of all foreigners in treaty relations with this old Hermit of the nations.

The recent war between China and Japan attracted the attention of the civilized world. It shook the dragon throne of China, and disturbed the conservative order of things throughout Asia, and even in Europe. The signs of the times are ominous of great changes among the nations, especially in the East. What these changes will probably be, we may not anticipate. Our young people should inform themselves as to international questions, and as to the political and moral condition of the world.

In addition to my own personal observations while in China, I have consulted the best authorities accessible to me. I have endeavored to give due credit where I have borrowed directly anything from an author. If in any case I have failed to do so, the reader will please believe it an oversight.

I am indebted to our Mission Rooms, and to returned missionaries, for most of the illustrations which embellish this volume —that is, for photographs from which they have been engraved.

W. G. E. C.

Nashville, Tenn., *May*, 1896.

# CONTENTS.

|  | PAGE |
|---|---|
| INTRODUCTION | 9 |
| I. ANTIQUITY OF THE CHINESE | 15 |
| II. GEOGRAPHY OF CHINA | 26 |
| III. THE POPULATION OF CHINA | 34 |
| IV. THE PEOPLE OF CHINA | 41 |
| V. THE LANGUAGE OF THE CHINESE | 55 |
| VI. THE LITERATURE OF THE CHINESE | 67 |
| VII. GOVERNMENT AND LAWS | 79 |
| VIII. THE DYNASTIES OF CHINA | 94 |
| IX. RELIGIONS OF CHINA | 103 |
| X. RELIGIONS OF CHINA (CONTINUED) | 118 |
| XI. RELIGIONS OF CHINA (CONTINUED) | 130 |
| XII. WORSHIP OF ANCESTORS | 144 |
| XIII. THE SCIENCES IN CHINA | 159 |
| XIV. ARCHITECTURE OF THE CHINESE | 173 |
| XV. THE DRESS OF THE CHINESE | 179 |
| XVI. DIET OF THE CHINESE | 187 |
| XVII. AGRICULTURE IN CHINA | 196 |
| XVIII. MANUFACTURES IN CHINA | 206 |
| XIX. SOCIAL AND DOMESTIC LIFE IN CHINA | 216 |
| XX. FESTIVALS AND AMUSEMENTS | 234 |
| XXI. SUPERSTITIONS OF THE CHINESE | 247 |
| XXII. CHRISTIAN MISSIONS AMONG THE CHINESE | 265 |
| CONCLUSION: THE PRESENT CONDITION OF CHINA | 283 |

## ILLUSTRATIONS.

|  | PAGE |
|---|---|
| A Mandarin of the Second Class | *Frontispiece* |
| Sedan Chair | 14 |
| The Great Wall | 25 |
| Chinese Cooper | 40 |
| Airing the Birds | 54 |
| The Six Styles of Chinese Characters | 59 |
| Chinese Band of Music | 66 |
| Trial Before a Chinese Court | 78 |
| Punishment of the Wooden Collar | 93 |
| Temple of Heaven, Peking | 102 |
| Buddhist Priest | 117 |
| Temple of the Five Hundred Gods, Canton | 129 |
| Ancestral Hall | 143 |
| Practicing Archery | 158 |
| Chinese Soldiers | 158 |
| Chinese Carpenter | 172 |
| Chinese Blacksmith | 172 |
| Chinese Tailor | 180 |
| Chinese Shoemaker | 183 |
| Street Restaurant | 186 |
| Chinese Cart | 195 |
| Tea-curing House | 202 |
| Chinese Loom | 205 |
| Reeling Silk | 205 |
| Chinese Artist | 211 |
| Embroidering | 211 |
| Bride and Bridegroom | 215 |
| A Bridal Procession | 226 |
| City Wall and Canal | 233 |
| Punishment in School | 246 |
| Traveling on a Wheelbarrow | 264 |
| Li Hung Chang | 282 |

# INTRODUCTION.

### BY REV. COLLINS DENNY, M.A.

A QUAINT application of the familiar proverb, "One good turn deserves another," is that a benefit conferred lays ground for the expectation of another benefit. It is certainly true that when one gives out of his resources what will be for the welfare of others, the act of giving tends to rouse in the giver an interest in those he benefits; and interest frequently rouses love, and love is accompanied by the feeling of obligation. The giver thus comes to feel himself the debtor to those for whom he has already done so much, and the payment of such debts is one of the most unalloyed pleasures of this life. The apostle to the Gentiles declares that he was debtor both to the Greeks and to the Barbarians, and the payment of his debt was doubtless one of the sweetest drops in his cup of joy. No true mother considers what her love impels her to do for her child a hardship. He who is Lord of all became the servant of all, and died for all, because he loved all.

Dr. Cunnyngham has spent many of the years of his long life in work for the young people, yet this book is evidence that he has not lost his interest in those for whom he has labored. These long years of work give him many qualifications for the preparation of a new book intended chiefly for young people, not the least of which qualifications is his increasing love for his beneficiaries—his desire to promote their welfare.

But Dr. Cunnyngham, who has planted so many of his days in the lives of young people, has special qualifications for the work he has undertaken. He spent nine years in China, studying the people, working for them and with them. It has been said that the reason some people wear only one eyeglass is because they see through their one glass a great deal more than they comprehend; and a man may spend a lifetime in a community and not thoroughly know the community. The knowledge a man brings back from a residence in any country depends very much on the man. In this instance the man is a Christian, a minister of the gospel, a former missionary; one who went to the people, lived among them, studied their language, yea studied them, that he might supplant their error with the truth of God. In addition to this long personal knowledge of the Chinese, Dr. Cunnyngham has not only been a close student of the literature relating to China and her people, but since his return to America he has also kept himself in close, living touch with many of the workers in that land. The book will be the best evidence that his residence in China and his close study of the literature of the subject qualified him to write a history of the people among whom he so long lived.

The subject of this book claims attention. It is a young people's history; but not a history of wars, of dynasties, of court gossip. It was a magnificent advance when historians presented the world with the results of their study, not of a ruler simply, but of a people. In this instance we are given the history of a people singularly ignored by the vast majority even of students of history, yet of a people from whom the world can learn many interesting and profitable lessons.

All of us have read of nations whose course we followed from their strong youth to their graves. One by one those nations we are wont to call ancient went out of existence, and this is so constantly repeated that we are not surprised to be told of the islander who shall in some future time sit upon the remnants of London Bridge and gaze wonderingly on the ruins of the city's great cathedral. We no more expect, until the exceptional case occurs, to find a nation ending indefinitely than we expect to find a white crow. It may startle us to learn that the Chinese have a history of a life unbroken for more than four thousand years; that this people, substantially as we now find them, looked down on the cradle of nations we call ancient, nations long since vanished. The Greeks were great, in some important points great enough to be our recognized masters; but they were not great enough to lay the foundations of their national life so firmly as to endure. The Romans were strong, their legions tramped the world almost at will; but they were not strong enough to maintain a national life as long as that of the Chinese. Some nations have gone down because hollow within they could not resist the pressure from without; and some have been destroyed because of internal conflagration. The Chinese show the world a nation not so hollow as to have been broken by the strongest pressure to which they have so far been subjected from without, nor so inflammable as to have been consumed by the fires kindled from within. The long life of this people commands our attention and presents us with a problem whose solution may be of the greatest profit to ourselves. Is their endurance due to some of the elements peculiar to their environment, or to their racial traits, or to some of the features of their dominant ideals? No single circumstance is ever the cause of an event; both the moving hammer and the whole stone must be included among the antecedents some of whose consequents are a broken stone and a hammer at rest. The long national life of the Chinese is a complex event whose cause must be an aggregate of different elements. Can we find the tough fibers of this strong cable that has enabled the Chinese to ride out the storms in which so many nations have been wrecked?

An isolated people, provided their territory be small and their numbers few, may escape for many years the disasters that break on the heads of others; but in the case of the Chinese we have a people whose territory is one of the most extensive of the earth, and a population far more numerous than any other nation. Surely students and readers cannot much longer ignore the Chinese; it is not to their credit that they have so long passed them by.

"The greatest thing on earth is man," because

he is truly not a thing, but a person with possibilities not yet fully calculated by our finite minds. If it be not correct to say the sole " proper study of mankind is man," it is true that man is a worthy study. Heretofore man has not been studied in all the variations of circumstances to which he has been subjected. He has not been looked at critically, lovingly, and exhaustively in what, from our point of view, are the narrower opportunities of Chinese civilization. But how can we expect to make valuable inductions about our race, or even complete statements of observations of the race, while we refuse to investigate carefully the phenomena presented by the millions in China? They lack many of the things esteemed by us to be necessities, yet from a worldly standpoint some of them may be called happy. Let the powers of the world to come take hold upon him, and without denationalizing him regenerate him, then who can doubt that the Christian Chinese may have as distinct a lesson for the world and as noble a work as the Christian Anglo-Saxon? A true appreciation of these strangers in the East will lead to a willingness to receive from them anything of good they may be able to contribute to the true development of the world, and to return to them what they lack of the greatest elements in our Christian civilization.

May the young who read this history become so interested in the wonderful people of whom it treats that when older they may help to solve some of the problems the Chinese present to the world.

Vanderbilt University, *April* 13, 1896.

SEDAN CHAIR.

(14)

# A YOUNG PEOPLE'S HISTORY OF THE CHINESE.

## CHAPTER I.

### ANTIQUITY OF THE CHINESE.

WE are indebted to the Arabs for the first definite information we have concerning China and its inhabitants. In A.D. 850, and also in A.D. 877, two enterprising Arabian travelers visited the eastern coast of Asia, and among other countries, then unknown to western nations, which they explored was the empire of China. They spent some months among that strange people, studying their language, customs, and manners, their arts and manufactures, and on their return to their own country reported what they had seen and heard. During their travels they kept a journal, which was afterwards translated and published. Their account of China and its people agrees so exactly with what we know of them to-day, though more than a thousand years have passed away, as to give great credibility to their narrative.

In 1274 the great Venetian traveler, Marco Polo, entered China and spent seventeen years at the court of the Mongolian conqueror of China, Kublai-Khan. His report of the country, the population, wealth, and resources of China, was received with incredulity by his countrymen, and by Europeans generally. These doubts have, however, long since given place to admiration for the simple and faithful statements of the honest and truthful Venetian.

Pope Nicholas, in 1288, sent John De Carvino as a missionary to China. He was the first successful agent of the Roman Catholic Church in the East, and a man of great learning and zeal. His descriptions of China and the Chinese confirm the reports of the Arabian travelers, of Marco Polo, and others who visited that country in the thirteenth and sixteenth centuries, showing that China has changed but little through the ages of her long national history. She is substantially the same to-day that she was three thousand years ago.

When western scholars first began their researches into Chinese history, they discovered that some native writers claimed a very great antiquity for their country, even tens of thousands of years. This fact was eagerly seized by European skeptics as casting discredit upon the comparatively recent account of Moses. They declared that Chinese history proved that " the Bible is unreliable;" that " the Bible history is contradicted by the authentic records of ancient nations;" that " according to Chinese chronology the people of China were laying the foundations of their empire at the time when, according to Moses,

God was creating the heavens and the earth; and that the Chinese husbandman was tilling his farm at the time Moses represents Adam as cultivating the garden of Eden,'' etc.

Subsequent and more careful investigation of the subject, however, showed that the Chinese divide history into three periods: '' The Unknown,'' '' The Fabulous,'' and '' The Known.'' '' The Unknown '' belongs to the age of the gods, and has no record in time—its events are known only to the gods. '' The Fabulous '' embraces the prehistoric period between the age of the gods and the appearance of the first man, or the age of the sages. The first period has no chronology, and no history. The second period is characterized as mythological, by reputable Chinese writers, in which appear the fabulous rulers: (1) The '' celestial emperor,'' who reigned forty-five thousand years; (2) His successor, the '' terrestrial emperor,'' who reigned fifty thousand years; (3) After these the '' human emperor,'' whose reign lasted only eighteen thousand years. The third period begins with the first real character in Chinese history, the Emperor Yu, and continues down to the present time.

It will thus be seen that the Chinese, like most other heathen nations, have a *mythological period* of indefinite duration, covering the unknown ages which passed away before the appearance of man on the earth; and a *chronological period*, beginning with the first recorded event in authentic history, and coming on down to the current year. No reputable Chinese historian has any more respect for the absurd legends of the mythological age than we have. It was these mythological fables that led the early students of Chinese history into the mistake of supposing that there were authentic records in China running back into the misty ages of antiquity far beyond the beginning of our biblical chronology. The European skeptics enjoyed but a short season of exultation over the friends of Moses and the Bible. It was soon discovered that Chinese history, so far from casting discredit upon the record of Moses, tends strongly to confirm it. The argument, therefore, against the authenticity of our Scriptures, based upon the supposed historical records of China, like a similar argument founded upon the fabulous legends of the Egyptians and Hindoos some years before, had to be abandoned by its advocates, and Moses is still read and believed by millions of intelligent and good people.

The first real character in Chinese history, according to the most reliable authorities, native and foreign, was the Emperor Yu, who began to reign somewhere about the year B.C. 2204. The exact date cannot be ascertained, for at that early day there were no written records, and the historians who subsequently wrote of the beginning of their national annals were entirely dependent upon tradition, a most unreliable and unsatisfactory source of information. The earliest authentic written history of the Chinese people belongs to the age of Confucius, B.C. 549; not that there was no written history, or what claimed to be history, before that age, but it is to the great sage that we are indebted for the first authentic and digested history of the Chinese people, their customs, manners, and institutions. The great Chinese historian, Chu-foo-tsz, next to Confucius, is an authority on all matters of ancient history. "From these and other native writers modern historians have gathered all they know about the early history of China, and they all agree in regarding the Emperor Yu as the first authentic historical character." *

"If, then," says Dr. Medhurst, "we consider Yu to be the first real character in Chinese history, and place the beginning of his reign at B.C. 2204, or one hundred and four years after the flood, about the age of Peleg, when the earth was divided, we shall find that it gives time for such an increase of the human family as would admit of emigration, and yet allow for China being in such a state of marsh as to require draining for the sake of cultivation, which service was ascribed to the labors of Yu. Thus the empire of China, when deprived of its fabulous and traditionary periods, is still very ancient. The Chinese must have branched off from the great human family immediately after the Dispersion (Genesis x.), and, traveling to the farther East,

---

* Medhurst: "State and Prospects of China."

settled down on the borders of the Yellow River, coeval with the establishment of the Babylonian and Egyptian monarchies."* Thus, ere Rome was founded or Troy was taken, before Thebes and Nineveh were erected into kingdoms, China was a settled state, under a regular form of government, with customs and institutions similar in many respects to those it now possesses.

If Confucius were to revisit his native land to-day, he would find things generally pretty much as he left them more than two thousand years ago. He could read the last book published, if not the last bulletin posted. He would find hundreds of thousands, if not millions, of scholars who could repeat *verbatim et literatim* all he ever wrote; and he would also find himself still enthroned as "the peerless and unapproachable master," whom millions worship at myriads of altars.

The question has been asked again and again, but never satisfactorily answered: "How is it that China has thus lived through so many centuries, successfully resisting the laws of national decay, while every other nation that began its course with her has long since disappeared from the face of the earth, or been so changed as to lose its national identity?" Babylon, Egypt, Nineveh, Greece, and Rome, once the contemporaries of China, lie buried in the dust of the dead past; yet China survives in all her original

---

* See Parke's History of China, 1588; Chinese Repository, Vol. X., No. 3.

integrity, the one lone monument of antiquity on the plains of time that has not been destroyed or dismantled by the hand of decay or the storms of revolution.

What has China done for the world to entitle her to such distinction among the nations? What promise does she give of service to mankind? Her great longevity is as much an historical enigma as the preservation of the Jews through so many ages of national vicissitude. But we know what the Jews have done for the human race. They have preserved through the dark centuries of the past a knowledge of the true God, his word and his worship, and above all they have given the world its Messiah. Besides, many believe that they are yet destined to bless the world as "the chosen people of God." China, on the contrary, has been atheistic and idolatrous, has dishonored God and despised his law. She has lived in wantonness and pride through all her generations, and in her self-sufficiency has hated and scorned all other nations. She has neither feared God nor regarded her fellow-man, and now in her withered old age still clings to the traditions and customs of her early days; she is still selfish and egotistical, arrogant and insolent toward other nations.

Some writers have attributed the great longevity of China to natural causes, such as "geographical position, the generally favorable climate, the average fertility of the soil, great facility of internal commerce," etc.* Some have attributed it to moral causes, such as the fact that the Chinese have never deified vice in any form; others, to the observance of the fifth commandment.

None of these suggestions seem to be entirely satisfactory. Other countries have enjoyed as great natural advantages as China, as friendly climates, as fertile soils, as good water, and all other favorable conditions, and yet they have not passed the average age of the nations. As to the moral causes—that the Chinese have never deified vice in any form. In this matter they can claim only a limited negative virtue, for they have enshrined in their hearts and practiced in their lives all that Bacchus and Venus represent. There is not a more sensual people on earth than the Chinese, their own writers being witnesses. There is not a sin mentioned by St. Paul, in the catalogue of vices enumerated in the first chapter of Romans, of which they are not guilty. I do not say all the Chinese are thus guilty, but the sins referred to are practiced more or less by them as a people.

That the Chinese do, in a sense, observe the fifth commandment is true—they do reverence their parents, and after their death they worship them; but they know nothing about the command of God requiring children to honor their father and mother, and do not do it as an act of obedience to God, but as an act of idolatry. They

---

* Sir John Davis.

have made reverence for their parents an occasion of sin. Ancestral worship is the most universal form of idolatry in China. All worship at the ancestral shrine, the old and the young, the great and the small, the rich and the poor, from the emperor on the Dragon Throne to the beggar in the street—all worship their dead ancestors. They may worship at no other altar, but all worship here. That this universal sin could become a reason why God should specially bless the Chinese as a nation, and preserve them through so many ages, is a species of logic I cannot indorse. Of all the obstacles in the way of the Christian missionary in China, the most formidable is ancestral worship. The Chinese will give up all other forms of idolatry before they will this. To neglect the tombs of their ancestors is an act of ingratitude and sacrilege at which they obstinately revolt.

That China is the oldest nation in the world there can be no reasonable doubt, but what causes have operated to preserve her through so many centuries we are unable to say. Revolution after revolution has swept over the land, and her dynasties have been changed twenty-five times, and two hundred and forty-three emperors have occupied the Dragon Throne; but still China remains substantially the same through all these changes that she was when Abraham was in Chaldea, or Joseph in Egypt. From the first emperor, Yu, to the present "year of grace" (1896) is four thousand and one hundred years. What great events in human history have taken place during these forty centuries! The Chinese were living where they are now, and quietly cultivating the soil, or fighting the "barbarians," when Israel marched out of Egypt; when God gave the law to Moses amid the awful scenes in Sinai; when David was king; when the Queen of Sheba visited Solomon; when Nebuchadnezzar took Jerusalem; when Alexander conquered Egypt; when America was discovered; and—to-day. We dare not predict anything for the future. Recent events have awakened a deep interest throughout the Christian world in the fortunes of China. War with Japan, internal commotions, foreign complications, and national imbecility seem to threaten the integrity of this ancient empire.

THE GREAT WALL.

(25)

## CHAPTER II.

### GEOGRAPHY OF CHINA.

THE present empire of China consists of five great divisions: Manchooria, Mongolia, Turkestan, Thibet, and the Eighteen Provinces, or China Proper. It is to the last that reference is usually made when speaking or writing of China. The others are provinces of great extent, but thinly inhabited, and of a low grade of civilization.

MANCHOORIA is the home of the Manchoo Tartars, a half-civilized and half-nomadic race, which has attracted the notice of foreigners chiefly because of its connection with China. The present imperial dynasty is descended from the Manchoos.

MONGOLIA lies immediately north of the Eighteen Provinces, and is a wild and desert country, consisting mainly of barren wastes. The inhabitants are roving nomads, who live in tents, and follow their flocks as they wander from place to place. They are devout Lamaistic Buddhists, fierce and fanatical.

TURKESTAN is situated in the northwestern borders of the Eighteen Provinces, and is inhabited by a settled Turkish race of Mohammedans. It contains the two celebrated cities of Cashgar and Yarkand, with several smaller cities.

THIBET is west of China Proper, and is inhabited

by a settled people, and is the headquarters of the Lamaistic form of Buddhism. The chief or high priest of this strange sect claims to be the incarnate Buddha. The capital of Thibet is Lassa.

These four great divisions of the Chinese empire are not inhabited by the Chinese, but by separate and distinct races, each race speaking its own language, and distinguished by its own peculiar national characteristics, customs, and manners. The Chinese speak of them as "outside the gates" —that is, outside of China Proper.

As the following pages will be devoted to a brief description of China and the Chinese people, no further notice will be taken of the provincial dependencies. The reader will please therefore remember that what is hereafter said about China refers to the Eighteen Provinces, or what is known as China Proper.

China is situated on the eastern coast of Asia, and contains about one-half of the whole territory of the empire. It is 1,474 miles in length, and about 1,355 miles in breadth, with a coast line of 2,500 miles. Its area is 1,399,609 square miles, "comprising within its limits every variety of soil and climate; watered by large rivers, and producing within its borders everything necessary for the support and comfort of man." *

Most of the great empires of Asia extend along its southern border, chiefly upon the shores of the Indian Ocean, and are bounded on the north by the

---
* "Middle Kingdom."

snowy peaks and pastoral wilds of Tartary. China, on the contrary, is situated on the Pacific, at the extremity of the Asiatic continent. The climate is generally salubrious, but, like all other countries situated on the eastern side of a great continent, is subject to extremes of heat and cold at different seasons of the year, not always corresponding with the degrees of latitude. Thus in the northern part of China the mercury often rises to 80° and 90°, and in the southern part frequently falls below zero in the winter.*

The whole surface of the country is diversified by mountain ranges, extensive plains, and undulating highlands. The lofty mountains which wall in the territory of Thibet and Tartary as they enter China sink down into elevations of moderate altitude. Two great rivers, the Yang-tse (child of the ocean) and the Wong-hoo, or Yellow River, corresponding to the two great rivers of our country, roll through the land from west to east, fertilizing extensive valleys, and furnishing the means of trade and travel for the millions of central and eastern China. There are other rivers that afford facilities for inland navigation, which, with the Yang-tse and Wong-hoo, give the people of China unequaled advantages in water ways. There are several lakes in China, but none of sufficient size or commercial importance to require special mention in this place.

The Grand Canal is a stupendous work,

---

* Sir John Davis: "Middle Kingdom."

equaled only by the Great Wall of China. By means of its connections with the rivers which flow into it, an almost entire water communication is completed across the country from Tien-Tsin, near Peking in the north, to Hang-Chow in the south, a distance of six hundred geographical miles, or "forty days' travel," as the Chinese estimate its length. It is sometimes said to be fifteen hundred miles long, but this is in Chinese miles, or *lee*, which is only about one-third of our mile. It is a great artificial river, costing millions of dollars to construct, and millions more to keep it in repair, and therefore entitled to a place in any description of the physical geography of China. It crosses the Yellow River about seventy miles from its mouth, and for ninety miles (between the Yang-tse and Yellow River) runs parallel with the latter, being carried through all this distance upon a mound of earth not less than twenty feet above the level of the surrounding country. The embankment of earth on each side of the canal is held in place by strong stone walls, or heavy earthen banks. Its depth varies from a few feet to several fathoms, and its width from one hundred feet to half a mile, according to the character of the country through which it passes. Stone abutments and floodgates are used to regulate the flow of the water, and occur at irregular distances according to the inequalities of the surface of the land. Hundreds of thousands of men were employed for an indefinite time on this great work. If the age in which this great national work was completed, and the character of the princes who planned it, be considered, few labors of human hands in any country in the world can be compared to it for extent and usefulness. The Grand Canal passes through some of the most beautiful scenery in China—rich valleys covered with highly cultivated farms, villages, hamlets, and cities, tea gardens, mulberry orchards, peach orchards, and all the variety of rural scenery to be found in any country. Again, it follows along the foot of an extensive mountain range, and winds its way through natural passes into the plains beyond, then on by Soochow, Nankin, and the "Golden Isle" to the terminus. As it approaches the province of Canton in southern China, its way has been cut by immense labor through a range of mountains which separates the province of Kiang-Si from Canton. This part of the work is said to have been done by an individual during the Tang dynasty, more than a thousand years ago.*

THE GREAT WALL OF CHINA deserves to be considered in a geographical point of view, and may therefore be noticed in this connection. It was built by the first universal monarch of China, more than two thousand years ago. It bounds the whole north of China, running along the frontiers of three provinces. The emperors of the Ming dynasty built an additional inner wall near to Peking on the west. The body of the wall consists

---

* Davis: "Middle Kingdom."

of an earthen mound, supported on each side by strong stone and brick masonry. The average height is about twenty-five feet. In some places it rises only a few feet above the level of the ground, as on rugged elevations where access to it is difficult, and in other places to fifty and sixty feet. The thickness of the wall at the base averages twenty-five or thirty feet, and at the top fifteen feet. Towers rise at frequent intervals, and are sometimes forty feet square at the base and thirty at the top. It ascends the highest mountains, and descends into the deepest valleys, crossing over rivers, and stretching its great length for fifteen hundred miles, more or less. Authorities differ as to the actual length of this artificial barrier, intended to protect the peaceable inhabitants of China from the incursions of the savage barbarians on their northern borders.

The coast of China, south of the Shan-Toong province, except at the mouth of the two great rivers and the well-known commercial harbors, is generally bold and rocky, and is lined throughout its whole extent, from Hainan to the mouth of the Yang-tse, with multitudes of islands and rocky islets. The interior of the Eighteen Provinces is divided into the mountainous, the hilly country, and the Great Plain.

The soil of China is generally fertile, and renders a rich return of harvests to even the unskilled labor of the ignorant natives. It is also well watered, and in some parts covered by noble forests.

In the more densely inhabited districts of the country, however, the forests have disappeared, and timber is consequently very scarce and costly, common firewood selling for two cents a pound in some parts of the empire. I do not remember, during my residence in China, to have ever paid less for the pine wood used for cooking. Originally the country was well wooded. We find there to-day, especially in the mountains, the oak in all its varieties, the black walnut, camphor tree, cedar, cypress, sandalwood, ebony, willow, chestnut, persimmon, hickory, hazelnut, mango, pineapple, orange, pear, peach, plum, apricot. Other trees and fruits common in the same latitudes all over the world are indigenous in China. The mulberry is extensively cultivated in the silk-growing districts, the leaves being used as food for the silk worms.

The bamboo is so universal, and used for so many purposes, that it might with propriety be called the national plant. It is cultivated about villages and hamlets for its beauty and as a shade tree. The tender shoots are used for food by the natives, and in taste so much resemble the young Indian corn of the West that foreigners regard them a delicacy, and in the season have them on the table as we do the "roasting ear." The old roots are used as material for ornaments, and are often exquisitely carved into many beautiful shapes. The stalks of the smaller species are used for canes, umbrella handles, spears, and many other purposes. The larger kind is used in building houses, making fences, chairs, tables, and for a variety of purposes too numerous to mention here. It is a beautiful growth, resembling in stem and foliage the larger species of cane that grows on our river banks, but much larger, attaining a height in some places of from fifty to seventy-five feet, and a diameter of four to six inches. The bamboo is in China what the palm tree is in India, a universal convenience.

There are many features of the physical geography of China which remind an American of his own native land. The two countries occupy nearly the same relative position on the map of the northern hemisphere. The coast lines, the mountain ranges, and the great rivers that flow through the land bear a general resemblance which the careful observer will not fail to notice. The general average of temperature is said to be a little lower in China than in America. The climate is therefore pretty much the same in both countries.

China is rich in minerals—iron, copper, gold, silver, and all other mineral products common to our country and Europe. There are immense coal fields, but imperfectly developed. In this, as in other things, the Chinese are without a knowledge of practical science, and therefore without the means of developing fully the rich treasures locked up in the vaults of nature. They deal only with the surface of things, and leave untouched the vast wealth that lies beneath.

## CHAPTER III.

### THE POPULATION OF CHINA.

THE population of China is estimated by foreigners anywhere from three hundred and fifty million to four hundred and twenty million. Recent statistics show that the larger number is probably the correct one, or at least nearest the truth. Whatever the exact figures may be, it is safe to say that one-third of the human race live in the dominions of the present Manchoo emperor of China.

It is difficult, if not impossible, for the human mind to conceive of the vast multitude of men, women, and children who live in China to-day. They are more than the combined populations of Europe, Africa, and the entire continent of America! Dr. Culbertson, in his little book on China, indulges his fancy in an attempt to array the millions of China in a procession, which in its grand march passes before the imagination of the reader. He says: "Suppose this mighty multitude to march in procession before you. Place them in single file, six feet apart, and let them march at the rate of thirty miles a day, stopping to rest on the Sabbath. Day after day you watch the moving column, and day after day the long march continues. The head of the column pushes on toward the setting sun. Now bridge the Pacific; bridge the Atlantic. And now the Pacific is crossed, but still the long procession moves on, stretching away over high mountains and sunny plains and broad rivers, through China and India and the European kingdoms, and on again over the stormy bosom of the Atlantic. But the circuit of the earth itself affords not standing room. The endless column must double upon itself, and double again and again, and shall girdle the earth *eighteen* times before the great reservoir which supplies these marvelous multitudes is exhausted. Weeks and months and years roll away, and still they come—men, women, and children. Since the march began the little boy has become a man, and yet on and on they come in unfailing numbers. Not until the end of forty-one years will the last one of that long procession have passed."

Some confusion in estimating the population of China has arisen from the fact that the whole empire is included in the estimate by one writer, and only the Eighteen Provinces by another. If we include all the people living under the present emperor of China, the immense population does not seem so incredible, though still largely beyond that of any other nation, ancient or modern. If we include in our estimate only the Eighteen Provinces, the number is, of course, less; but the bulk of the population of the whole empire live in China Proper, and are Chinese. Some writers have questioned the larger estimates of the population of China because, they say, so many millions could not find room to stand on the limited area, and certainly could not obtain subsistence. The fact remains, however, that these millions do find standing room and enough to eat. China could double her population and still have room and food enough. Her territory is vast, and the productions of the soil almost unlimited. Besides, she has an inexhaustible supply of fish in her rivers, lakes, and canals, with an extensive seacoast, giving her access to the boundless treasures of the ocean. China is rich enough in material resources to take care of her immense population, and to maintain an extensive export trade with other nations.

The stranger who visits China is impressed by the large number of populous cities thickly scattered over the land, and by the numerous villages that surround these cities. Take, for example, the district in which the city of Shanghai is situated. It contains no less than thirty large cities and towns within a territory not larger than some counties in Virginia—a territory twenty-seven miles long and twenty-six miles broad, with a population of several million. The city of Soochow, some eighty miles from Shanghai, has a population of two million, while the surrounding country is covered with cities, towns, villages, and hamlets. About twenty-five miles from Shanghai is a city of probably five hundred thousand inhabitants, and not far from it several cities of one hundred thousand people. So it is all over the more densely populated parts of China. In the Eighteen Provinces there are one thousand seven hundred and twenty districts, with a thousand cities, ranging in population from one hundred thousand to three hundred thousand, and one three million. Peking, the capital, has three million; Hang-Chow and Canton, more than one million each. The great city of Woo-Chang, with its two neighboring cities, has four or five million.

The Chinese swarm everywhere: in cities, towns, villages, and hamlets; in all the open places of the country; on all the highways and byways; on the land, on the water, on mountains, and in the valleys. "They are always near you; they are on your right hand and on your left hand, and in whatever direction you look they are always in sight." They are an industrious people, always busy, always moving. Even the beggars pursue their calling with a persistent business air. On every hand the scenes of a busy life meet your eye. If you would escape from the noise and babble of the multitude, you must retire to the solitude of the mountains. Everywhere around you, in the more populous places, are the abodes of the living and the tombs of the dead.

The cities of the dead occupy much space, and often intrude upon the abodes of the living. The poor cannot always afford to bury their dead, and therefore keep them in their houses, or place them in some open space, until they can pay the expenses of a cheap burial, or leave them thus to decay in the open air. Of course such scenes are witnessed only about large cities, where land is very expensive, and where the very poorest of the people live and die.

Dr. Williams says in regard to the credibility of the larger estimates of the population of China: "The Chinese people are doubtless one of the most conceited nations on earth, but with all their vanity they have never bethought themselves of rating their population twenty-five or thirty per cent. more than they suppose it to be, for the purpose of exalting themselves in the eyes of foreigners or in their own. Except in the case of the commissioner who informed Lord Macartney, none of the estimates were made for or intended to be known by foreigners. The distances given in miles between places in Chinese itineraries correspond very well with the real distances; the number of districts, towns, and villages in the departments and provinces, as stated in their local and general topographical works, agree with the actual examination so far as it can be made. Why should their censuses be charged with fraud and gross error, when, however much we may doubt them, we cannot disprove them, and when the weight of evidence derived from actual observation rather confirms them than otherwise?"

If all who have lived and died in China were enumerated, figures would fail to express the vast sum. The necropolis of China greatly exceeds the present population of the world. And they are still increasing, and still dying.

The great problem which the Christian philanthropist should contemplate with profound concern is the moral and religious condition of the millions of China. We see the long procession, which Dr. Culbertson so graphically describes, on its solemn march to eternity, going down to the grave without hope. How little relatively has been done by the Churches of Christendom to save them!

CHINESE COOPER.

## CHAPTER IV.

### The People of China.

THE original seat of the Chinese people was in the great plain of northern China, in what is now known as the Province of Chih-li, not far from Peking, the present capital of the empire. How they came to be there it is impossible to ascertain. Chinese historians seem satisfied with the assertion that their people have always lived where they are now, the only place on the face of the earth fit for the residence of the highest order of man. They say "China is the only civilized country in the world; all other people are barbarians," who have no history worth recording, and who live on barren islands off the coast of China. Of course there are Chinese who know better, but such is the popular belief, founded on immemorial tradition.

The average Chinese looks upon Europeans and Americans as belonging to an inferior race. To him there are, and always have been, but two classes of men in the world—the Chinese and the barbarians. It is a little amusing to know that the half-naked creature that performs the most menial offices for you, and would serve you in any capacity for a few cash, nevertheless regards you as his inferior. The same arrogance and silly self-conceit which have led Chinese historians to ignore all people besides themselves, or to characterize them as barbarians unworthy of notice, has induced entire silence in regard to their own origin. The first man that ever lived was a Chinese, and from him the race has descended. Where he originated we are not informed. "He made the sun, moon, and stars, and chiseled all things out of the vast masses of granite floating in space. He was assisted in his stupendous labors by the dragon, the phenix, and the tortoise." After eighteen thousand years of toil " the heavens rose, and the earth spread out and thickened; and all things being made, the first man died for the benefit of his handiwork." After his death his head became mountains, his breath winds and clouds, and his voice thunder, etc.* Such was the first Chinese man. How grotesque these absurd myths! How greatly inferior to the Greek fables, or Egyptian symbols! How sublime and beautiful the account which Moses gives of the creation of the heavens and the earth, of the first man, and the beginning of human history!

The Chinese are doubtless the descendants of Shem, the eldest son of Noah. It is not unreasonable to suppose that the sons of Noah, learning from their father that the world was without inhabitants, and guided by a divine impulse, began to colonize as soon as they began to form families. The first three centuries would be time enough for some of them to reach the eastern

---

*"Middle Kingdom."

coast of Asia and settle down in the land of Sinim, or China. They may have passed from Persia through central Asia and down the Yellow River to the Great Plain. From this locality they spread south and west as they increased in numbers until they covered the plains of central and southern China, where they have made their permanent home. Thus, from the beginning of their national history, the Chinese have been isolated, and left to develop a unique character, uninfluenced by association with other people. Out of the line of conquest, away from other great nations, they have escaped the dreadful scourge of foreign wars, and being superior in numbers and intelligence to the rude tribes on their borders, have lived in comparative peace, and in great national prosperity. Their peculiarities as a people may be attributed to the character of their indigenous civilization. Foreign influences have had little or nothing to do with forming their political and social institutions. They have borrowed nothing from other nations; have no models but those of their own ancestors, and have therefore studied themselves, imitated themselves, and repeated themselves, generation after generation, through forty centuries.

The physical characteristics of the Chinese have been thus described by Dr. Williams: "They are in person between the agile Hindoo and the muscular and fleshy European; their form is well built and symmetrical. Their color is a brunette, or sickly white, rather approaching to a yellowish tint than a florid, but this yellow has been much exaggerated; in the south they are swarthy but not black, never becoming as dark as the Portuguese. The hair of the head is lank, black, and coarse. It is always black and defiant. The eyes are invariably black, and apparently oblique. The cheek bones are high, and the outline of the face invariably remarkably round. The nose is rather small, much depressed, and nearly even with the face at the root, and wide at the extremity; lips thicker than Europeans; the hands are small, and the lower limbs better proportioned than among any other Asiatics. The height is about the same as that of Europeans."

Between the provinces of Kwang-se and Kwei-chow in central China there are several tribes called Meaou-tsze, or "children of the soil," who have maintained their independence of the government for hundreds of years, perhaps thousands, for little is known of their history. They are supposed to be the aborigines of that part of the country. In many respects they are unlike the Chinese; they are really a different race of people, and by many believed to be older than the Chinese. This, however, can hardly be true, for all history points to the Chinese as the original inhabitants of central China. The Meaou-tsze are a strange race of hardy and brave nomads, living in a wild and barbarous state in the midst of Chinese civilization. During the Taiping rebellion they were said to sympathize with the rebels, though they took no part in the war. They hate the present Manchoo dynasty.

There are provincial peculiarities that distinguish the inhabitants of one province from another, but they are not sufficiently marked to affect the uniformity of the national character; they are all Chinese who live within the Eighteen Provinces, except perhaps the Meaou-tsze, to whom reference is made in the preceding paragraph; and the following delineation of character is therefore intended to apply to all the Chinese.

A just estimate of Chinese character, by a foreigner, is perhaps an impossibility: we have not the information concerning the private, domestic, and social life of all classes necessary to a full and fair judgment. Official intercourse with them discloses only their diplomatic shrewdness and utter want of principle. All is artificial and false. To deceive and mislead—to conceal their real sentiments and hide their ultimate purpose—seems to be a fundamental rule of action when dealing with the representatives of foreign governments. Commercial intercourse with them displays the same characteristics, modified by the laws of trade. As to the domestic life of the people, we know comparatively little. They are shielded from the vulgar gaze of foreigners by doors that remain barred and bolted against us, except in the case of the very poor and the few families connected with Christian missionaries. We now and then hear of a foreigner who has been admitted within "the gates of a home," but not to the inner apartments.

Our knowledge, therefore, of the real character of the Chinese is imperfect, not only because limited to mere superficial intercourse, but because what we see is artificial, and much of it false. "Things are not what they seem"—in China. Such at least was my experience during a residence of nine years in their midst. I speak of the people as a mass, not of the Christian converts, for they are few in number and not representatives of their heathen countrymen. They have abandoned the "old ways," and adopted the habits of a better life.

I shall notice first the more commendable traits of Chinese character; and secondly, those which are characteristic of the worst side of their nature. They have been misrepresented by two classes of writers; one extolling them as excelling the rest of the world in all the qualities which constitute national greatness, especially in the science of good government, in practical and useful knowledge, and even in morality. We are told that "the Chinese have demonstrated that Christianity is not necessary to the highest civilization, for they have attained the most advanced culture without any knowledge of our Scriptures or creeds." Another class of writers denounces them as among the lowest specimens of the human race, hardly above the beasts of the field. Both estimates are erroneous, for the Chinese are not the highest order of civilized men, nor are they the lowest order of animal creation.

*The permanency* of Chinese institutions certainly speaks well for them. If they have not solved the great problem of human government, they have succeeded in preserving intact through thousands of years, far beyond that of any other nation, their form of government and their national institutions. The successive irruptions of northern barbarians have never destroyed or materially modified their original civil constitution. China is to-day politically what she was four thousand years ago.

The Chinese are an industrious, quiet, peace-loving people. They reverence age, and consider themselves bound to absolute obedience to parents. Thus the young are under the control of the oldest surviving heads of families, and the ignorant and inexperienced are guided by the more mature judgment of their elders. This habit of subordination, and the consequent control of their ruder passions, tend to render crimes of violence less frequent than in almost any other country. Under real or supposed injury, however, they are sometimes revengeful and cruel, and not at all scrupulous as to how they avenge themselves. They are kind to the poor, and in a measure benevolent. Buddhism has exerted a good influence upon them in this respect. There are homes for the aged and infirm who have no living relatives to care for them, or means to take care of themselves. I once saw an asylum for homeless and friendless cats, founded by a devout Buddhist woman. There are foundling asylums, free dispensaries where medicine is furnished to the poor, in some of the large cities of the empire. In seasons of famine and of general public distress, wealthy Chinese give liberally for the relief of the suffering. Heathenism has, however, nowhere provided asylums for the comfort of the unfortunate; and we must therefore infer that the asylums in China are the fruit of Christian teaching, perhaps of the early Romish missionaries. The Chinese are not naturally humane or philanthropic.

They have attained a good degree of security of life and property. The various classes are linked together in a remarkable manner by the diffusion of education and the personal rights to property, the equality of competition for office, the just reward which industry receives, a general distribution of food and clothing, and the protection and security of home life. Even their idolatry, degrading and abominable as it is, is less coarse and sensual than that of most other heathen nations. They have never deified the beastly and inhuman vices which characterize some pagan systems of religion. The public respect shown to common decency in dress and manner is commendable.

The marriage relation is respected in China, and though polygamy exists throughout the empire, no man can legally have more than one wife. The children are trained to obedience, to respect age, to good manners, and to be industrious. They are also taught to reverence the gods from their infancy, and to worship them at home and in the temples. In China, as in other countries, the women are more religiously inclined than the men, and the mothers are therefore the religious teachers of the children. Corrupt and debasing as Chinese heathenism is, it is better than atheism, and many of the lessons inculcated are far above the practice of the average devotee.

The Chinese appear to the foreign observer to be a cheerful and contented people, and in a measure they are. Their cheerfulness, however, is more seeming than real. They are phlegmatic in temperament, cold and dull, and therefore not easily excited. Besides, they are fatalists, and believe that "whatever is to be will be" in spite of all that men may do. They also believe that the state of things surrounding them as a people is the very best that could possibly be; hence their intense conservatism, which gives to their conduct and conversation the appearance of contentment. They bear misfortune with apparent fortitude, but it is rather a hopeless apathy than a cheerful submission. It is a silent acquiescence in the inevitable. It must be, then why complain or struggle against it?

Other commendable qualities of the Chinese might be mentioned, but the limited space assigned to this subject forbids further remark at present. They have another side to their character, which must be noticed in this connection.

The inordinate self-conceit of the Chinese may not be classed among their gross vices, but it is certainly a very offensive trait of their character. They claim too much. We may allow them to be a very great people, but we cannot permit them to monopolize all the wisdom and knowledge in the world, and to be the only civilized nation in existence. We must protest against the arrogance with which they assert their claims to superiority. Their supercilious treatment of foreigners is unpardonable.

Among the objectionable traits of Chinese character which an Englishman or American observes with special disapproval is their want of truthfulness. They seem to prefer any form of speech that does not require a plain, straightforward statement of the truth; and this is not confined to their intercourse with foreigners, but is common among themselves. This feature of their character has done more to lower them in the eyes of Christendom than perhaps any other. Recent events connected with the murder of missionaries in China, and the official investigations which followed, furnish new evidence of the utter mendacity of the people and their rulers. They misrepresented the facts in every instance. Diplomatic and official intercourse with foreign nations has always been characterized by the same vice on the part of the

Chinese government. Social and commercial life is disfigured by this hateful sin; and what seems to us strange, they feel no shame when detected in a barefaced falsehood.

The moral teachings of Confucius have done much, doubtless, to regulate and restrain the coarse and savage nature of the Chinaman, but his system provides no radical remedy for sin. It may give an outside varnish to character, but cannot change the heart. Christianity alone has power to thoroughly purify the fountain of life so that the stream may be pure.

Thieving is common in China. Indeed, it is reduced to a science, and the thieves are regularly organized, having their chiefs and subordinate officers, with rules and regulations for their government. They are perhaps the most expert pickpockets in the world. Many amusing stories are told of their adroitness. They are severely punished when brought before the mandarins, if they happen not to have "a friend at court;" but it is said that the police find it to their interest to ignore their existence. Lying and cheating are common among merchants and tradesmen. Every man is supposed to be competent to take care of his own interests.

There are many other vices of the Chinese which might be enumerated, but I have said enough perhaps in this connection to serve my present purpose. They are not the only sinners in the world. We can see much evil without going to

China. And we should not forget that the Chinese exhibit many commendable qualities. Another thing also we should bear in mind: they are heathens, ignorant of the divine morality of the gospel, and without the inspiration of lofty motives or noble ideals. Their civilization belongs to a rude and barbarous age. Their historic models were semi-barbarians, and they have learned little or nothing from other nations.

The Chinese present a strange mixture of character. If there is something to approve in them, there is much to condemn. They have glaring vices, and they have commendable virtues. We find ostentatious kindness and secret hatred, civility and rudeness, partial invention and servile imitation, industry and waste, sycophancy and independence, strangely blended. We must not judge them too severely, but remember always who they are—pagans, Asiatic pagans, Mongolian Asiatic pagans. The Chinese who have come to our country are not fair specimens. They belong to the grade of common laborers and small tradesmen.

There are provincial differences among the inhabitants of the Eighteen Provinces, in language and manners, which mark them as distinct from one another as the Latin races of Europe. This fact renders any general characterization of the Chinese people exceedingly difficult. A description of the people of Canton, in southern China, for instance, would require considerable modification to make it applicable or just to the people of Shanghai, in eastern China; and so of all the provinces widely separated. I lived for years in daily contact with the people of Shanghai and vicinity, and I studied them and their institutions, their customs and manners, as carefully as I could, and have embodied the result of my experience in this chapter. My views are doubtless somewhat colored by the local peculiarities of the people among whom I lived, but I have tried to inform myself, in regard to the general character of the people as a whole, and trust I have not entirely failed to do them justice, imperfect and unsatisfactory as this brief sketch necessarily is. The task is a difficult one.

AIRING THE BIRDS.

# CHAPTER V.

## THE LANGUAGE OF THE CHINESE.

### *I. WRITTEN LANGUAGE.*

THE Chinese language, written and oral, like the people who speak it, is peculiar. It stands alone among the many forms of human speech which exist in the world. Sir John Davis says of it: "The highly artificial and philosophic structure of this singular language entitles it to the attention of all intelligent persons, as a part of the history of the human mind. But it has other powerful claims to notice, from being the medium through which at least *four hundred millions* of mankind, occupying countries which exceed the united extent of all Europe, communicate their ideas." The people of China Proper, Manchooria, Mongolia, Turkestan, Bucharia, Thibet, Cochin-China, Loo-Choo, Japan, Corea, and the inhabitants of Farther India, all use the Chinese written character more or less. Some suppose that five hundred millions of people can be approached through this one medium of communication. The only characters which approach it in this respect are the *Arabic numerals*, common to all Europe. This advantage, which pertains only to the Arabic numerals, belongs to the whole Chinese written language. The words are monosyllabic, and the characters symbolic, neither having changed materially for many centuries. In fact, the written language has no history since the death of Confucius. The generations since his day have strictly followed his example, and thus become a nation of servile imitators. Forsaking the dictates of their genius, or the teachings of reason, they have degraded themselves to the condition of mere copyists, regarding the sages of antiquity as the schoolmen of the West did the Bible and its scholiasts, as not only true, but as containing all truth, so that anything not taught by them was rejected as false and useless. The text of the ancient classics has always been regarded by the Chinese with as much superstitious jealousy as the Jews affect for the sacred language of their law. Some palpable typographical errors have been carefully perpetuated because found in the original copies.

Another circumstance has operated to prevent changes in the written language of China: it has no affinity with any other known tongue, and from its peculiar structure is incapable of incorporating or naturalizing foreign words. Having no facilities for the study of any foreign literature, Chinese scholars have been shut up to the study of themselves only. The student has had but one model, and this is the standard by which his proficiency in all literary work is tested. Close imitation of the ancients, therefore, has always been a condition of literary or scholastic success in China. The intellect of the nation has been thus cramped and distorted by this foolish system of repression. It has deprived their literature of all originality, and consequently of all intellectual vigor.

The foregoing observations apply strictly only to the classical language and literature in China, for the biographies, novels, state papers, religious tracts, etc., exhibit a considerable variety of style. Many are written with a colloquial freedom very unlike the square, stiff style of the classics; but all works that claim any literary merit conform more or less to the fixed iron standard. Business men, who as a rule make little pretension to scholarship, have adopted a style of writing suited to the nature of their occupation. Many of them can keep books, and conduct a business correspondence, who cannot read intelligibly a page of the ancient classics. Letter-writing has not been cultivated beyond a brief formal communication practiced by school teachers with their pupils, and the commercial correspondence of business men.

Chinese writers, unable to trace the history of their written character, have adopted the shorter method of referring all to supernatural agency. They say when the first characters were invented "the heavens, the earth, and the gods were greatly agitated. The inhabitants of hades wept at night, and the heavens rained down ripe grain." When the first symbols of a written language were employed nobody knows. "The primitive characters of the Chinese language are derived from the natural or artificial objects of which they were at first the rude outline. Most of the original forms are preserved in the treatises of native philologists, where the changes they have undergone are shown. The number of objects chosen at first was not large; among them were the symbols for the sun, moon, hills, objects in nature, animals, etc." These original pictures were doubtless very rude, but they served to recall the objects they were intended to represent, and thus formed the foundation of a pictorial language which was gradually developed into a written character.

The written characters have been arranged by Chinese philologists into six classes, corresponding to our black letter, the Roman, the Italic, the written, and the running forms. The Chinese running hand might very easily be taken for an alphabetic character. It would be interesting to illustrate these remarks by examples if we had the necessary type; but as these cannot be procured, it will perhaps be as well to leave this part of the subject undeveloped. See cut on opposite page.

The mode of printing first adopted by the Chinese has not been materially changed. The first step in the process is to write the characters on thin paper, ruled with lines to separate the columns and the division of the pages, two pages always being cut upon one block, and a heavy double line surrounding them. The title of the book, chapter, and paging are in a column between the pages, and when the leaf is folded through this column the characters appear on the edges and partly on both pages. This renders it easy to re-

THE SIX STYLES OF CHINESE CHARACTERS.

fer to the chapters and pages. Marginal notes are placed on the top of the page; comments occupy the upper part, separated from the text by a heavy line. Sometimes two works are printed together, one running through the volume on the upper half of the leaves, and the other on the lower half, the two divided by a line.

When the leaf is fully written out, just as it is to appear in the book, it is turned over and pasted on a block of wood face downward to invert the page. The block is usually made of plum or apple tree, about half an inch thick, and planed smooth on both sides. The paper when dried is carefully rubbed off of the block with the finger moistened with water or saliva. The impression of the characters remains on the block as distinctly as on the written sheet of paper. "The cutter," as he is called, with a small sharp chisel removes the wood around the characters, leaving them in relief. The block then looks like a stereotype plate, and is ready for the printer, who lays it on a pile of soft paper supported by a bench or stool, and "inks" it with a small brush made of the fibrous bark of the palm. He then places a sheet of "printing paper" on the block, and another sheet on that, and with one or two sweeps of a soft brush makes a complete impression of the characters on the block. The sheets when printed are placed in the hands of the binder, who folds and stitches them, and the work is done. Chinese books are of all sizes, from quartos twelve or fourteen inches square down to 32mos. The price varies, according to the size and character of the book, from one cent to one dollar a volume. The government exercises no censorship over the press other than a prohibition to write about the present dynasty. Authors and publishers are not protected by any form of copyright.

Books are hawked about the streets as newspapers are with us; circulating libraries are carried from house to house upon movable stands, and booksellers' shops are numerous in all the large cities and towns. Tracts on various subjects, especially on moral and religious topics, are sold, or distributed gratuitously. The Buddhists have been, in many parts of the country, very active in tract distribution since missionaries began their labors among their people. Placards, posters, "dodgers," and all sorts of advertisements, are spread on walls, pasted on boards, or scattered over the face of the country. They are of all sizes and designs, some in bright colors, some large, some small, some illustrated. The Chinese have a sense of the ludicrous, and lampoons, pasquinades, and caricatures are common; nor is anyone below the emperor spared. Some of these caricatures of foreigners are very amusing.

As to the structure of the Chinese language I shall say but little. A few words, however, in regard to the grammar may interest my youthful readers. Rémusat, in his great work, gives a brief summary of the principles of Chinese grammar. He says: "In every Chinese sentence, in which anything is understood, the elements of which it is composed are arranged in the following order:

The subject, the verb, the complement direct, and the complement indirect. Modifying expressions precede those to which they belong: thus, the adjective is placed before the subject, or complement, the substantive governed before the verb that governs it; the adverb before the verb; the preposition incidental, circumstantial, or hypothetical before the principal proposition, to which it attaches itself by a conjunction, expressed or understood. The relative position of words and phrases thus determined supplies the place often of every other mark intended to denote their mutual dependence, their character, whether adjective or adverbial, positive, conditional, or circumstantial. If the subject be understood, it is because it is a personal pronoun, or that it is expressed above, and that the same substantive that is omitted is found in the preceding sentence, and in the same quality of subject, and not in any other. If the verb be wanting, it is because it is the substantive verb, or some other easily supplied, or one which has already found place in the preceding sentences, with a subject or complement not the same."

In the absence of all inflection, the relation of words to each other in a sentence can be fixed only by their collocation. The verb, for instance, must always precede its object and follow its subject. The plural number is indicated by an affix, or by repeating the noun; but both are unnecessary when the number is prefixed—as, three men.

The genitive or possessive case is generally denoted by the sign " tsz " succeeding the noun like our s. The comparison of adjectives is marked by affixes. The tenses of verbs are indicated by auxiliaries, etc.

### II. SPOKEN LANGUAGE.

Under this head little can be said, unless we examine the local peculiarities of the many dialects into which the colloquial language of China is divided. This would have little interest for the common reader.

It is difficult to say how many dialects there are in the Eighteen Provinces. First, because it is not easy to distinguish the peculiarities of pronunciation of one dialect from another; that is, it is difficult to say whether what you hear in one province is merely a variation in the pronunciation of a familiar word, or another word altogether. It is, secondly, difficult to say how many dialects there are, because in remote mountain districts, and other obscure localities, the people are in a semi-barbarous state, and neither they nor their language well known. Some native authorities suppose there are sixty different dialects, others say thirty-six, and some only twenty.

Added to these causes, and perhaps the most radical influence in dialectical variations, is the fact that China originally consisted of several independent tribes, or nations, all of one common stock, but as different in many of their local customs and manners as if they were politically independent sovereign states. This has tended to preserve and increase the differences in the provincial dialects. Again, some are more and some less cultivated, as there were educated men in some localities and not in others. Among the more intelligent inhabitants of cities the language has approached more nearly the court dialect, while in the rural districts it has suffered the deteriorating effects of ignorance, modified, as all languages are, by the habits and occupations of the people. The written language never having been colloquial, the dialects have as a consequence been neglected by the educated classes.

The dialects of China, like the written language, are monosyllabic, and limited in most instances to a few hundred words, but by a system of tones may be and are multiplied to an almost indefinite extent, furnishing a colloquial medium of communication sufficient for all ordinary purposes. The Chinese, especially the lower classes, are fond of gossip, and while away many an hour in hearing and telling stories. Ghost stories have a peculiar fascination for the ignorant, who revel in the weird and improbable. A sense of humor is also common among all classes of Chinese, and the grotesque and absurd are used sometimes with great skill to embellish an otherwise prosy narrative. This fondness for story-telling has had its influence upon the language of the common people.

As a sample of colloquial Chinese the following translation of the Apostles' Creed, in the Shanghai local dialect, is here given, furnished me by Mrs. J. W. Lambuth:

### SING KYUNG.

Ngo siang toh yer ieh ko zung, yang yang nungker ko ya, sier sz Sau zung koong *Te<sup>n</sup>* lau *De*.

Ngo siang sing e-ko-toh yangne-tsz *yasoo ke-tok*, ngoo ne ko *Tsu*.

Ngo siang sing *Mo-le-a* waytsz *Sun Ling* ko nungker lau yang *yasoo* lay ko.

Ngoo siang sing yasoo la *Pay-la-too* tsoo qway ko sz-yer ser tsz na*n*, ding la seh sz-ha-long, se tsz lau tsong; la te sa*n* nyih long, E tang se-wyung tong-tsoong weh tsay lay ko; Ngoo siang sing *yasoo* song tsz *Te<sup>n</sup>* lau zu la yang yung wung ker ko *Ya*, sier sz *Tung*, ko yer ba*n* ba*n*, her ser yau tang e qway tsay lay, lau sung mung weh-la, lau se-la-ko nyung.

Ngoo siang sing *Sung Ling, Sung-koong way,* Sung doo ko seang toong, lau tswer nyih ko nyau-so.

Ngoo siang sing myoh-sung ko weh tsay lay, lan yoong yoong yer yer weh la.            *A Mung.*

5

CHINESE BAND OF MUSIC.

## CHAPTER VI.

### THE LITERATURE OF THE CHINESE.

CHINESE literature is divided into four great sections: first, the sacred or classical books; second, history and biography; third, works on science and art; fourth, light literature, novels, plays, romances, and poetry. Some idea of the extent of this literature may be formed from the imperial catalogue, which contains the titles of twelve thousand works, with tables of contents. They have twenty-four complete histories of the empire, anterior to the present Manchoo dynasty, which began to reign (in 1644) two hundred and fifty years since. Material for the history of this dynasty is being collected to be used at some future time.

The department devoted to art and science contains a variety of works highly esteemed by the learned natives, but of little intrinsic value. Treatises on morals, etiquette; familiar dialogues by their great sage, Confucius; books on the military art, on agriculture, etc., are to be found in every gentleman's library, and on many subjects discussed they display sound, practical views—mixed, it is true, with much that is absurd. The Chinese are a reading people, and the respect they show to men who have excelled in literary work speaks well for the popular taste. No man (theoretically) who is not a scholar can hold any office in the empire above that of a policeman.

Chinese literature has been greatly enriched by Protestant and Romish missionaries. The Bible has been translated into the language of Confucius, and parts of it into the local dialects, especially in southern and eastern China. Many religious tracts, treatises on astronomy, geography, and mathematics, have also been published in the language. The labors of Christian missionaries in heathen lands will one day be appreciated by the world, not only because they have delivered nations and tribes of men from the horrors of social and domestic barbarism and brought them into the family of civilized Christian nations, but because they have added more than any other class of men to the general knowledge of mankind. They have been the pioneers of civilization in almost every land under heaven. They have explored the wilds of Asiatic and African jungles, at the peril of their lives, in search of lost and unknown tribes, that they might teach them the way of life. They have been the first to bring to the knowledge of the Christian world the rich treasures of undeveloped mines of wealth. What does Africa not owe the immortal Livingstone? What does the world not owe him? What does China not owe Morrison, Milne, Medhurst, and the many others, great and good men and women, who have given their lives to redeem her millions from heathen darkness?

They labored not for wealth or fame, but that they might carry the glad tidings of the gospel to dying men. The Master will not forget them in the day when he makes up his jewels.

### *THE CHINESE CLASSICS.*

The limits assigned to this volume will not permit even a brief sketch of the Chinese system of education. I have therefore chosen to place under the head of "The Chinese Classics" such facts and observations as I suppose will illustrate the methods of literary training which have been pursued for centuries in China. Education is not esteemed in that country for its own sake so much as for the distinction which it confers, and the political advantages and opportunities which it affords. No man can hold any high office who is not a classical scholar; and as office is the goal of every man's ambition whose social position allows him to aspire to any place of honor among his fellow-men, education, at least in name, is eagerly sought. It is therefore interesting to know what Chinese education means—what it is. The one essential condition, fixed by law, is that the student shall pursue a classical and historical course of study, and must pass an examination before the board of examiners. If successful, his name is placed on the bulletin board in the magistrate's office, and he is recognized as entitled to a place among candidates for literary honors. There are four literary degrees. The candidate is examined for each degree, and may fail to obtain any one or all. Some men attend the annual examinations for the first degree until they are seventy-five years old.

Much fraud and corruption is said to exist in the examinations, and in the distribution of honors by examining boards. In one year more than twenty thousand forged diplomas were sold.

The Chinese have private schools, common schools, high schools, academies, colleges, and universities. What proportion of the people can read is a difficult question to answer. Many more in the cities can read than in the country. Some can call over the names of characters who have no idea what the characters mean. Thus one can read what he does not understand, but others hearing him may understand perfectly what he is reading. Tradesmen, mechanics, and country gentlemen endeavor to give their sons an education that will fit them for business, and enable them to mix pleasantly with general society. Such an education does not, however, entitle a man to be called a scholar, or to claim any of the privileges awarded to literary men.

The classical or sacred works consist of nine, or what the Chinese call the " Four Books," and the " Five Canonical Works." In the course of a regular education the Four Books are first studied and committed to memory, and afterwards the others. The texts of these books, without notes, are comprised within a small compass.

The numerous commentaries, however, which have been added to the text swell the whole to a formidable bulk. The cheapness with which Chinese books can be produced brings them within reach of everyone who can read.

1. The first of the Four Books, the *Ta-shoo*, shows that all government must originate in self-government, for if a man cannot govern himself he cannot govern others. Personal virtue, according to the teachings of Chinese philosophy, forms the foundation of all good character, and without it no man is fit to be a ruler, whatever his genius or learning may be. Morality is thus made the chief element in a sound statesman or politician. (See Chapter VII.)

2. The second of the Four Books is called the "Infallible Medium," and inculcates the wisdom of moderation in all things. Whatever misfortunes a man may suffer, he should always be "equal and moderate;" never haughty in a high station, nor base in an humble one.

3. The third book of the series is the record of the conversations and sayings of Confucius, reported by his disciples; a sort of Boswell's biography of the sage. It is very interesting, and consequently exceedingly popular among Chinese scholars.

4. The fourth book is the work of Mencius, a celebrated sage, who lived about one hundred years after Confucius. This book exceeds in size all the other three, and is devoted to the great

theme of Confucius—benevolent and just government.

5. Confucius was either the author or compiler of the Five Canonical Books. The common name for these books is *king*. The first is called the " Book of Sacred Songs," a collection of about three hundred short poems.

6. The second of the series is an imperfect and obscure book, which the Chinese do not claim to understand fully.

7. The third of this series is the " Book of Rites," and is considered as " the foundation of the present state of Chinese manners, and one of the causes of their uniform unchangeableness."

8. The next in the series is a history of his own times, and of those which immediately preceded them, by Confucius. It is supposed to be the only *original* work of the great sage. His design appears to have been to warn the rulers of the country of the dangers which threatened the stability of the government.

9. The last is a mystical book, which some consider a very ancient theory of creation, and of the changes which are constantly occurring in nature.

The foregoing imperfect sketch of the books known as the Chinese classics may serve to give the reader some idea of their character, and therefore of the mental food upon which the Chinese have been feeding for ages. There is much good advice, much practical wisdom, taught in these ancient books, but there is no reference to an Unseen Power to whom all men are accountable for their actions; no reference to a future state of rewards and punishments. All is of "the earth, earthy," limited to time and to the affairs of this life.

### SPECIMENS OF CHINESE POETRY.

The earliest literature of the Chinese were the songs and ballads, collected by Confucius into a single volume known as the "Book of Odes." These odes date back to a very early period in Chinese history. Confucius had a collection of three thousand, from which he selected and edited three hundred and eleven, arranged under four heads: (1) "National Airs," (2) the "Lesser Eulogies," (3) the "Greater Eulogies," and (4) the "Song of Homage." To this collection he gave the title of *Shoo-King*, or "Book of Odes."

Through most of these odes there breathes a calm and patriarchal spirit of simplicity. There are few sounds of war, little tumult of the camp, but, on the contrary, a spirit of peaceful repose, of family love, and of religious feeling. We have brought before the mind's eye the lowly cottage, where dwells a family united by the bonds of affection and duty. Their food is the produce of the soil and the spoils of the chase. The highest ambition of the men is to excel as archers and charioteers, and their religious worship is the same as that, untainted by Buddhism or any other form of philosophical teaching, now practiced at the imperial temples of heaven and earth, by the emperor only as high priest.

The following selections are taken from the "Book of Odes." Who translated them I do not know; nor do I know how true the translation is to the original. The Chinese commentators tell us that the following ode is intended to depict a domestic scene, in which an industrious wife impresses on her indolent husband the necessity of early rising, and exhorts him to make virtuous and respectable acquaintances:

> "Get up, husband, here's the day!"
> "Not yet, wife, the dawn's still gray."
> "Get up, sir, and on the right
> See the morning star shines bright.
> Shake off slumber, and prepare
> Ducks and geese to shoot and snare.
>
> "All your darts and line may kill
> I will dress for you with skill.
> Thus a blithesome hour we'll pass,
> Brightened by a cheerful glass;
> While your lute its aid imparts
> To gratify and soothe our hearts.
>
> "On all whom you wish to know
> I'll girdle ornaments bestow;
> And girdle ornaments I'll send
> To any one who calls you friend;
> With him whose love for you's abiding
> My girdle ornaments dividing."
>
> —*Book of Odes, Ode 8.*

Another specimen is taken from a poet of the Wai dynasty, A.D. 620. The title of this poem is, "The Lament of a Soldier on a Campaign:"

> On the hilly way blows the morning breeze,
> The autumn shrubs are veiled in mist and rain.
> The whole city escorts us far on our way, providing us
> With rations for a thousand *li*.
> Their very worst have those Fates done. Ah me!
> How can I be saved? There is naught more bitter than an early death. Do not the gods desire to gain perpetual youth?
>
> As sorrow and happiness, so are fortune and misfortune intermingled. Heaven and earth are the molds in which we are formed. And in them is there nothing which does not bear significance?
>
> Far into the future looks the sage, early striving to avert calamity. But who can examine his own heart, scrutinize it by the light of heaven, regulate it for his present life, and preserve it for the old age which is to come?
>
> Longer grows the distance from what I have left behind me: my trouble is greater than I can bear.

This may be poetry, but it looks and sounds very much like wretched prose. The translator has not, perhaps, done the original full justice. The Chinese language is not well adapted to poetic expression.

One of the most ancient pieces in the "Book of Odes," the date of which may reach three thousand years, has reference to a rich and powerful suitor, who carries off the bride who had already been engaged to an humble rival. The allusion is to some robber bird, which, like the cuckoo, deprives weaker ones of their homes; and the translation of this antique specimen may serve to show the similarity that pervades the tone of human sentiment in the most distant ages and countries:

The nest yon wingèd artist builds
  The robber bird shall bear away:
So yields her hopes th' affianced maid,
  Some wealthy lord's reluctant prey.

The fluttering bird prepares a home
  In which the spoiler soon shall dwell:
Forth goes the weeping bride, constrained,
  A hundred cars the triumph swell.

Mourn for the tiny architect,
  A stronger bird hath ta'en its nest;
Mourn for the hapless, stolen bride,
  How vain the pomp to soothe her breast!

*CHINESE APHORISMS.*

What cannot be told had better not be done.

The torment of envy is like a grain of sand in the eye.

For old age and withered flowers there is no remedy.

Riches come better after poverty than poverty after riches.

Great wealth comes by destiny, moderate wealth by industry.

The error of one moment becomes the sorrow of a lifetime.

A great man never puts away the simplicity of his childhood.

Who swallows quick, can chew but little: so it is with learning.

Better be a dog in time of peace than a man in a season of anarchy.

Borrowed money makes time short, working for others makes time long.

You cannot take two skins off of one cow. There is a limit to extortion.

The gem cannot be polished without friction, nor man made perfect without affliction.

The man who aims at excellence will rise above mediocrity, but the man who aims at mediocrity will fall below his aim.

Let every man sweep the snow from before his own door, and not trouble himself about the frost on his neighbor's roof.

A rash man is fond of provoking trouble, but when the trouble comes he is no match for it; a clever man turns great troubles into little ones, and little ones into none at all.

The fish dwell in the depths of the waters, and the eagles in the sides of the heavens: the one, though high, may be reached by an arrow; and the other, though deep, may be caught with a hook. But the heart of man, though only at a foot's distance, cannot be known.

TRIAL BEFORE A CHINESE COURT.

## CHAPTER VII.

### Government and Laws.

ALTHOUGH revolution after revolution has swept over China during the many centuries of her national existence, and although she has changed her dynasties more than twenty times, and internal convulsions have shaken her throne to its foundations, she has never changed her form of government. Other nations and tribes, partially civilized, have been added by conquest to her national domain, yet all have been blended politically into one homogeneous mass, and forced into obedience under one scheme of civil administration. In this, as in many other things, China stands alone in her unique greatness, the wonder of the world. The line on the chart of history that marks her place among the nations is the only line that runs with unbroken continuity entirely across the chart.

The Chinese government is modeled after the natural constitution of the family, the emperor being the *father*, and the people his *children*. The obligations of patriotism are founded upon the filial relation, and all the duties of good citizenship are enforced by the same principle. One of their sacred books says: " In our general conduct, not to be orderly is to fail in filial duty; in acting as a magistrate, not to be careful is to fail in filial duty; in the intercourse of friends, not to be sincere is to fail in filial duty; in arms, and in war, not to be brave is to fail in filial duty." The idea of filial reverence and obedience due to parents is applied to all the senior members of the family, and the duty to reverence the aged is enjoined upon the same principle. Old age is honorable, reverenced by all classes, and recognized by the government. When a man in China reaches the age of eighty years, he is reported to the emperor, and a yellow robe—the imperial color—is bestowed upon him as a mark of imperial respect, on the presumption that he must have lived a virtuous life to have been thus favored by heaven.

As an example of the manner in which the government sometimes punishes a violation of filial obligations, the following story is related by Sir John Davis: "A man and his wife had beaten and otherwise severely ill-used the man's mother. This being reported by the viceroy to Peking, it was determined to enforce in a signal manner the fundamental principle of the empire. The very place where the offense occurred was anathematized and made a curse. The principal offenders were put to death; the mother of the wife was bambooed, branded, and exiled for her daughter's crime; the scholars of the district for three years were not permitted to attend the public examinations, and their promotion was thereby stopped; the magistrates were deprived of their office and banished. The house in which the offenders dwelt was dug up from the foundations." An imperial decree ordered that proclamation of the facts in the case be made throughout the empire, that "if there be any rebellious children who oppose, beat, or degrade their parents, they shall be punished in like manner." The local officers are required to read publicly on the first and fifteenth of the month "the sacred instructions" addressed to the people, in which their duties are set forth so that they may not be ignorant of what they ought to do.

The Chinese government, as it now exists and has existed for thousands of years, is the result of an historical evolution of the patriarchal idea as set forth in the ancient classics. The father of the principal family became the chief of the clan or tribe, and thus as the tribe increased and families branched off and new tribes were formed, the head of the senior or parent tribe became the recognized chief of all the tribes, and as the tribes increased to a nation the first or principal chief became the supreme ruler, the king or emperor of the whole nation. This principle of patriarchal supremacy, and the corresponding obligation of filial reverence and obedience, form the basis of the whole system of Chinese political economy. All the machinery of government has been adjusted to this one supreme idea, namely, the right of the parent to govern the child, and the duty of the child to render implicit obedience to the parent. By this simple and natural law the millions of China have been governed for thousands of years.

In recognition of the exalted position the emperor occupies, and the absolute power with which he is clothed, the people have exhausted the vocabulary of oriental hyperbole in attempts to describe in suitable phrase the greatness and glory of his "celestial majesty." They call him "The August and Lofty One," "Son of Heaven," "Sire of Ten Thousand Years," etc. He only has a right to worship heaven. Thus exalted, flattered, worshiped, the fountain of all power, rank, honor, and privilege, we would naturally infer that he was in all things absolutely irresponsible; but not so. The people expect and require him to rule according to the published laws of the land; and if he does not, they know how to assert their rights even against the throne. More than once the officers of the government have been assassinated when attempting to execute imperial edicts that were oppressive; and no attempt was made to punish the actors, because the body of the people defended them. "There exists among the Chinese a strong democratic element which finds expression and scope for action in their municipal regulations. Every ward in China has its elders, its public hall, where the people meet for the transaction of business, and its placards are public manifestoes, in which the popular sentiments of the people are boldly expressed; and both unpopular officers and offensive acts of government are sometimes criticised and denounced with irresistible logic and overwhelming ridicule"

(Mackay). These elders are chosen by the people, and their authority is generally ultimate in adjudicating any case brought before them. The government regards them as the patriarchs of the people, and holds them responsible for the acts of the ward in which they reside. If a riot occurs in the ward, the elders are expected to have the guilty parties arrested and handed over to the government for punishment. If they neglect or refuse to do so, they are held to be themselves the offenders, and are dealt with accordingly. This makes them careful to maintain good order in their wards, and aids very materially in the administration of the law throughout the land.

"The general government" of China, using our American terminology, consists of the emperor, the cabinet or privy council, the general or public council, and under these the six boards.

1. *The Board of Civil Office* has control of all the officers in the civil service, and assists the emperor in the administration of the government; regulates the order of rank, the bestowment of rewards and punishments upon faithful and unfaithful officers.

2. *The Board of Revenue.* This board has charge of the census, and regulates the levying of duties, taxes, etc. It also has charge of salaries, and the internal commerce of the empire.

3. *The Board of Rites* examines and directs concerning the performance of the five kinds of ritual observances, and makes proclamation there-

of to the whole empire. All rites and ceremonies are under the supervision of this board.

4. *The Board of War.* This board has the government and direction of all the military officers, military operations, military examinations, and all that belongs to the army.

5. *The Board of Punishments* has the government of all punishments throughout the empire. The emperor exercises clemency toward criminals, or enforces the law rigidly, according to the recommendations of this board.

6. *The Board of Works* has the oversight of all public works in the empire, and is also charged with the duty of providing the funds necessary for carrying on all public improvements.

In addition to the "general government," which embraces the whole empire in the scope of its administration, there are provincial or state governments provided for the Eighteen Provinces into which China Proper is divided. Each of the provinces has its governor-general, lieutenant-governor, treasurer, judge, literary chancellor, and commissioners of rice and salt. Every province is divided into counties, townships, and wards. At the head of each township is a magistrate, with his assistant constable, etc. It would not interest my readers, perhaps, to go farther into details in regard to the local government. Enough has perhaps been said to give some notion of the general structure of the Chinese system of government.

The nobility of China include the members of

the imperial house and clan, of which there are twelve orders. These orders, as a body, are destitute of power, land, wealth, office, or influence. They inherit the empty titles, which are not practically worth as much as the old clothes of their ancestors.

The civil officers of the empire are chosen by the emperor from the literary class alone, usually from those who have obtained the three degrees of bachelor of arts, master of arts, and doctor of laws. The very highest civil officers are taken from the class of scholars who have received the fourth or highest degree of literary honors. This secures the best talent in the empire to fill the government offices, and constitutes the only real aristocracy in China.

### LAWS OF CHINA.

During my residence in China I studied as carefully and as thoroughly as I could the government, the religion, the domestic and social life of the people, their customs, superstitions, etc., but not their laws. I visited occasionally their courts, heard cases tried, and in a general way picked up some idea of Chinese law, but not enough to enable me to write intelligently about it. I will therefore take the liberty of quoting and condensing from Dr. Williams's "Middle Kingdom" so much as will give the reader a general idea of the character of Chinese laws, and the manner of executing them.

The Chinese code is called "The Statutes of

the Great Pure Dynasty," and contains all the laws of the empire. These laws are classified under seven general heads, namely: general, civil, fiscal, ritual, military, criminal, and those relating to public works.

1. *The General Laws* consist of instructions as to the principles which should guide the officer in the construction and application of the laws.

2. *The Civil Laws*, consisting of twenty-eight sections, are divided into two books, one of which refers to the system of government, the other to the conduct of magistrates.

3. *The Fiscal Laws* contain rules for enrolling the people for succession and inheritance, for regulating marriages between different classes of society, for guarding granaries, treasuries, etc.

4. *Ritual Laws.* This department contains instructions concerning sacrifices, worship of ancestors, etc.

5. *Military Laws.* These laws provide for the protection of the imperial palace, for the government of the army, the defense of the coast, the management of the imperial cattle, etc.

6. *Criminal Laws.* This division contains one hundred and seventy sections, and is the most important part of the whole code. It relates to robbery, treason, homicide, murder, quarreling and fighting, abusive language, disobedience to parents, bribery and corruption, forgery, etc.—a miscellaneous list of offenses which fill pages of the statute books.

7. The seventh section contains laws regarding the weaving of interdicted patterns, repairing dikes, construction of government buildings, etc.

Dr. Williams regards the Chinese code of laws as upon the whole humane, just, and reasonable, but he admits that the execution of the criminal laws is often cruel and barbarous in the extreme. The tortures sometimes inflicted upon prisoners by coarse and brutal underlings, in order to extort money, or to gratify a fiendish love of cruelty, surpass anything reported of ordinary savage invention. We will have occasion to refer to this subject again, and shall not add further details at present.

---

In addition to what has been said in the foregoing pages concerning the government and laws of China, a few general observations upon the administration of the government and the execution of the laws may not be irrelevant in this place.

In order to appreciate, even in the least degree, the immense difficulty of holding together in any sort of harmony the four hundred millions of human beings under the scepter of the present emperor of China, we must consider the miscellaneous character of these millions; that they are not all Chinese, but the inhabitants of Manchooria, Mongolia, Turkestan, and Thibet. These are brought under the general administration of the one government with the inhabitants of the Eighteen Provinces of China Proper. How has this been done? Let those answer who can. China is the only nation in the history of the world that has accomplished such a miracle of government for any length of time, not to say for thousands of years!

Not only is the population of the empire of China composed of different nationalities, speaking different languages, with peculiar customs and manners, religions, traditions, and race antipathies, but the mixed mass is still further complicated by arbitrary class distinctions recognized by law and social custom. The following classifications are fixed by law: "First, natives and aliens; the latter class includes the unsubdued mountaineers and aboriginal tribes still living in the empire, races of boat people on the coast, and all foreigners living in the country, each of whom is subject to particular laws. Second, conquerors and conquered, having reference almost exclusively to intermarriages between Manchoos and Chinese. Third, freemen and slaves. Every native is allowed to purchase slaves and retain their children in servitude; and free persons sometimes forfeit their freedom on account of their crimes, or sell themselves into bondage. Fourth, the honorable and the mean who cannot intermarry without the former forfeiting their privileges; the latter comprise, besides aliens and slaves, criminals, executioners, police runners, actors, jugglers, beggars, and all other vagrant or vile persons, who are in general required to pursue for three generations some honorable and useful employment before

they are eligible to enter literary examinations."\*
There are also eight privileged classes, but only
the nobility can avail themselves of these privileges with any profit.

This great mass of humanity, thus diversified in
individual and national character, is no better and
no worse than the average man under the same
grade of civilization. The Chinese are not more
easily governed than other Asiatics. They are, as
a people, seditious, turbulent, covetous, and ambitious. There must therefore be something, not
only in the theory of government, but in the policy
and method of its administration, by which the
central government at Peking can keep a strong
and steady hand on every part of the vast political
machine, so as to direct all its movements. Our
knowledge of details in regard to the practical
workings of the central and provincial governments
is so imperfect that we cannot venture upon even
a probable explanation of the problem. We have
the results in the history of the great Chinese empire, but how these results have been attained we
do not understand.

Some facts, however, connected with the practical administration of the government may interest
the reader. We have seen how the democratic
element is incorporated into the ward system of
China. The deliberations and manifestoes of the
ward meetings are recognized by the emperor as
a part of the machinery of government. The sys-

---

\* Williams's "Middle Kingdom."

tem of mutual responsibility, which runs through every department of society, renders local disturbances of any kind, especially any interference with government officials in the discharge of their duty, a very serious matter. The locality where an offense is committed, no matter of what grade, is held responsible for it, and the elders of that particular ward must arrest the offenders and hand them over to the government.

The law forbids any man to hold office in his native province; besides preventing all intrigue when it would most likely succeed (among his own people), this law sends the office-seekers to Peking, where they come under the eye of the censors, whose business it is to scrutinize their fitness for office. Moreover, no officer is allowed to marry in the territory under his control, nor own land in it, nor have a son or brother or near relative holding office under him; and he is seldom continued in the same station or province more than three or four years. Local interests of any kind are supposed to be unfavorable to a faithful discharge of official duty. Theoretically, nepotism is impossible in China; practically, it exists throughout the empire.

Chinese officials are not at all without reproach in the matter of personal and official integrity. One of the censors in his report to the emperor says: "Among the magistrates are many who, without fear or shame, connive at robbery and deceit. Formerly horse-stealers were wont to conceal themselves in some secret place, but now they openly bring their plunder to market for sale. When they perceive a person to be weak, they are in the habit of stealing his property, and then returning it to him for money, while the officers, on hearing it, treat it as a trivial matter, and blame the sufferer for not being more cautious. Thieves are apprehended with warrants in their possession, showing that when they were sent out to arrest thieves they took advantage of the opportunity to steal for themselves."

While there are corrupt men in office in China, as in other countries (some not pagan), there are also good men, men who love justice and mercy, and who deal uprightly with their fellow-men. The moral teachings of Confucius are followed as faithfully by many Chinese officials as the precepts of the Bible are observed by officers of Christian governments. That there is much official corruption in China, from the imperial cabinet down to the lowest petty office, no well-informed native or foreigner doubts. Recent riots in China, in which several missionaries were murdered, were instigated by the mandarins for political purposes. The *literati* of China are haters of foreigners, and do all they can to keep alive the national prejudice against them. They inflame the minds of the ignorant masses by horrible stories, and thus assist the officials in exciting riots and murderous assaults on quiet and unoffending missionaries. The presence of missionaries and their teachings are a rebuke to the shameful lives of the mandarins and *literati*, and the people are not slow to see that the conduct of their rulers is a disgrace to the position they occupy.

It is not too much to say that the present government of China is thoroughly corrupt. The rulers are cruel, covetous, and oppressive. They need a higher civilization. The old forms remain as they were, but there is no life in them, no health, nothing but decay and death. What Western powers will do remains to be seen.* There is no question as to what the Church ought to do. Now is a crisis, not only with China politically and religiously, but with the Churches of Protestant Christendom. The Chinese need the gospel more now than ever before, if possible, and the obligation of Christians to send it to them is correspondingly increased. Western nations are increasing their armaments in the Chinese seas; the Church should increase its working force in China.

---

* This was written in November, 1895.

PUNISHMENT OF THE WOODEN COLLAR.

## CHAPTER VIII.

### THE DYNASTIES OF CHINA.

PERHAPS no part of Chinese literature is so little interesting to the average foreigner as the historical.* It is simply a dry record of the succession of dynasties, and the reigns of many sovereigns with unpronounceable names. China has had no connection with the rest of the world until during the last few hundred years, and other countries have taken little more interest in her affairs than if she had been located in the moon instead of being an inhabitant of our planet. We feel no sympathy with the dull record of the past dreary centuries through which she has lived. Even the wars of China fail to interest us. We are comparatively indifferent as to her political fortunes. Perhaps this is an unconscious retaliation for the supercilious manner in which the Chinese have treated other nations. I think the sympathies of the civilized world were with the Japanese in the recent war between the two countries.

A full, consecutive history of China would be an impossibility. The data for such a work do not exist. Many Chinese writers have attempted what they call history. There is one work of three

---
* A distinguished writer places Chinese historians at the bottom of the list of writers.

hundred volumes of this character, but it is after all only a prosy record of events, and not a history.  There is no logical order or philosophical sequence in the bald details, nor any attempt to explain events, or to trace them to their causes.  Sir John Davis says of Chinese history: "There is a continuous history of China, from the earliest ages down to the end of the Mongolian Tartar dynasty, called the 'Twenty-one Historians,' consisting of nearly three hundred volumes stitched with silk—yet we search in vain for anything beyond a barren chronicle of facts and dates.  Trains of reasoning and lessons of political philosophy can scarcely be looked for in a country the theory of whose government has always been despotic, however tempered by other circumstances.  'Instead of allowing,' observes Mr. Guetzlaff very correctly, 'that common mortals had any part in the affairs of the world, they speak of the emperors who then reigned.  They represent them as the sources from which the whole order of things emanated, and all others are mere puppets who moved at the pleasure of the autocrat.  This is truly Chinese; the whole nation is represented by the emperor, and absorbed in him.'"

Of course, with such a theory to guide them, no history of the nation could be written by native historians, or any reliable data furnished for future use.  The despot whom the historians feared, as did the people, would not permit any record of events which did not tend to magnify and exalt him and his administration. There could therefore be no true history of rulers or people under such circumstances. We are left with the barren annals of century after century, recorded by timid and time-serving writers, from which to gather the facts and events of four thousand years of Chinese history. Hence I have said a full and consecutive history of China is an impossibility. The data for such a work do not exist.

I have said thus much as introductory to what may appear to my youthful readers as a very dry and uninteresting sketch of the *Dynasties of China*. Such a sketch could not be well omitted. If it is not easy reading, it may be valuable for reference.

The reader will remember that in the first chapter, on the "Antiquity of China," we decided that the Emperor Yu was the first real character in Chinese history, and that he began to reign about the year B.C. 2204. Some writers place the date of his reign much earlier, even as early as B.C. 2800; but this would carry him back into the mythological period, of which there is no record. I have condensed for present use the "summary of Chinese history" as given in Williams's "Middle Kingdom." It is as follows:

1. The Hai Dynasty, founded by Yu the Great. This dynasty existed for four hundred and thirty-eight years, or from B.C. 2204 to B.C. 1766, under seventeen monarchs. Among the contemporary events of importance was the call of Abraham,

Jacob's flight into Mesopotamia, and Joseph's elevation in Egypt; also Jacob's arrival in Egypt.

2. THE SHANG DYNASTY followed the Hai Dynasty, and continued four hundred and forty-four years, under twenty-eight sovereigns, down to B.C. 1122. The principal contemporary events were the exodus of the Israelites, B.C. 1648; their settlement in Palestine; Othniel, Deborah, Gideon, Samson, and Samuel were judges in Israel.

3. THE CHAN DYNASTY lasted eight hundred and seventy-three years, under thirty-five monarchs, down to B.C. 249, the longest of any recorded in history. The principal contemporary events were the accession of Saul as king of Israel; taking of Samaria; David's reign; Rehoboam, taking of Jerusalem; death of Nebuchadnezzar; accession of Cyrus; return of the Jews; battle of Marathon; accession of Alexander; the conquest of Egypt by Alexander, etc.

4. THE TSIN DYNASTY. This dynasty began in B.C. 249, and lasted only three years.

5. THE AFTER TSIN DYNASTY, B.C. 246 to 202. This dynasty lasted only forty-four years. In this period of oriental history all the East was disturbed by wars and commotions, and in the West a similar state of unrest and strife existed.

6. THE HAN DYNASTY came into power in B.C. 202 and continued until A.D. 221, a period of four hundred and twenty-three years. It was divided into two dynasties, called the Han and the Eastern Han. During this period of Chinese history the

conquest of the Western world by the emperors of Rome established that great empire as "mistress of the world." The great events of this period were the advent of our Lord, his ministry and death, with the establishment of the Christian Church.

7. THE AFTER HAN DYNASTY began A.D. 211, and continued forty-four years under two princes. Under this dynasty the country was divided into three principalities. The first comprised all northern China, and was the most powerful of the three.

8. THE TSIN DYNASTY was founded by an ambitious general of the house of Han. He ascended the throne in A.D. 265, but ruled only over the western half of the country, and was engaged in constant warfare with the petty states that refused submission to him. Four emperors of this house ruled over China for fifty-two years.

9. THE EASTERN TSIN DYNASTY, successor to the last dynasty, reigned one hundred and three years under eleven princes. Buddhism and the doctrines of Confucius were dominant in this age. It was said that "children of concubines, priests, old women, and nurses administered the government."

10. THE SUNG DYNASTY was founded by a general who commanded the armies of Tsin. Displeased with the incapacity of his master, he caused him to be strangled, and placed his brother on the throne, who resigned for fear he should meet the

same fate. The general then seated himself on the throne in A.D. 420.

11. THE TSI DYNASTY was founded by Kauti, but he enjoyed the imperial honors but four years. He was followed by four princes, who reigned only a short time. The dynasty lasted only twenty-three years.

12. THE LIANG DYNASTY. Woo-ti, the first emperor of this dynasty, reigned forty-eight years. He was a great devotee of Buddhism, and like Charles V. retired to a monastery, but was persuaded to resume his crown. He, however, employed his time in teaching the doctrines of Buddhism to his courtiers. The dynasty ended in A.D. 557.

13. THE CHIN DYNASTY began to reign in A.D. 557. Three brothers reigned most of the time during this dynasty. The kingdom of Wei ruled over all northern China from A.D. 386 to 534, under eleven monarchs. It was finally separated into Eastern and Western Wei, and other smaller states.

14. THE SUI DYNASTY. This dynasty was weak and dissolute. The last ruler of the dynasty resigned in favor of Li Yuen, A.D. 618.

15. THE TANG DYNASTY. This celebrated line of rulers began their sway in peace, and during two hundred and eighty-seven years governed China wisely. They were probably the most civilized and enlightened monarchs of their age. Europe was suffering under the ignorance and

degradation of the middle ages. Twenty monarchs reigned during the two hundred and eighty-seven years this dynasty lasted.

16. AFTER LIANG DYNASTY. The last prince of the Tang dynasty was forced to abdicate, A.D. 907, and a struggle ensued against the usurper who seized the throne. After a reign of six years he was murdered by his brother, who reigned for sixteen years, and was slain by a Turkish general. Thus ended the dynasty, A.D. 923.

17–21. THE FIVE DYNASTIES, from 907 to 960. These short-lived houses are known in Chinese records as the "Five Dynasties."

22. THE SUNG DYNASTY began to reign in A.D. 970, after the turmoil and strife of the "Five Dynasties" were ended, and reigned until A.D. 1127, or one hundred and fifty-seven years.

Then followed the SOUTHERN SUNG DYNASTY, from A.D. 1127 to 1280, under nine emperors. After this the YUEN DYNASTY, founded by the great Mongolian, Kublai-Khan. This dynasty lasted eighty-nine years, when the Mongols were expelled. THE MING DYNASTY followed, and held the reins of government for two hundred and seventy-six years. The present dynasty, known as the TSING or PURE DYNASTY, came into power A.D. 1644, and has ruled China from that date down to the present day. The rulers are Manchoo Tartars. How well they have governed China does not enter into the design of this book to inquire in this place.

I have thus run rapidly through the long list of dynasties, which may interest some of my readers. It amounts to little more than the political calendar of the government. If I had space, it might be more interesting to give some account of the military character and wars of the Chinese, but I must desist.

TEMPLE OF HEAVEN, PEKING.

## CHAPTER IX.

### Religions of China.

#### *THE STATE RELIGION.*

ALTHOUGH no hierarchy supported by the state has ever existed in China, no body of priests has ever been able to rise to power and influence, or create a caste like the Brahmans of India, yet there is a state religion of very ancient date. It does not consist of doctrines which are to be taught, learned, and believed, but of rites and ceremonies to be observed. It is entirely a bodily service, and its ritual is contained in the statistics and code of the empire. The objects of worship are chiefly things, although *persons* are also included. There are three grades of sacrifices—the "great," the "medium," and the "inferior." The objects to which the great sacrifices are offered are four: heaven, earth, the great temple of ancestors, and the gods of the land and grain. The medium sacrifices are offered to the sun, the moon, the *manes* of deceased emperors and kings, Confucius, and the ancient patrons of agriculture and silk weaving; the gods of heaven and earth, and the passing year. The inferior sacrifices are offered to the ancient patrons of the healing art, and the spirits of deceased philanthropists, eminent statesmen, martyrs to virtue; to clouds, rain, wind, and thunder; the five cele-

(103)

brated mountains, four seas, and four rivers, famous hills, great water courses, cannon, flags, and many other things. The state religion is said to be greatly corrupted from its original simplicity. The emperor is the high priest, and renders homage to these objects of worship in person. When he worships heaven he wears blue robes, in allusion to the color of the sky; he wears yellow when he worships the earth, red when he worships the sun, pale white for the moon, etc.

"The state religion of China," says Dr. Williams, "is a mere pageant, and can no more be called the religion of the Chinese than the teachings of Socrates could be termed the faith of the Greeks." It is, however, connected with the sect of Confucianists, and all its members are men of literary distinction. It might with propriety be called "the sect of the learned," having the writings of Confucius as its sacred books. Confucius said little about religion, and his followers imitate his example in this as in other matters of opinion.

There exists but one temple in China dedicated to the worship of heaven, and one to the worship of the earth—both of them at Peking; and there the great sacrifices at the solstices are annually offered up by the emperor with much imperial pomp. One of the temples is situated east of the city, and the other west of the city. The whole system of worship is simply an imperial show—a materialistic display of gross idolatry.*

---

*See chapter on Chinese Worship.

## CONFUCIANISM.

Notwithstanding Confucianism is here placed under the general head of " Religions of China," it is not, strictly speaking, a religion at all, but rather, as Sir John Davis says, "a system of philosophy in the department of morals and politics;" yet it is not a system of philosophy merely, for it has a ritual and objects of worship, and is so far a religion. This makes it difficult to classify it. As the name Confucianism has been given to the whole system, and has been placed by all writers on the subject so far as I know under the general head of the " Religions of China," I shall so designate it. The other religions of China are Buddhism and Taoism. We may characterize the three systems as *ethical*, *metaphysical*, and *materialistic*. Confucianism addresses man's moral nature, discourses on virtue and vice, and the duty of obeying the dictates of conscience. The basis of the whole system is the duty of filial piety, hence the worship of ancestors, etc. Buddhism is metaphysical. It appeals to the imagination. Its gods are personified ideas; it denies the existence of matter, and concerns itself only with ideas. In other words, it is a form of idealism. Taoism is materialistic. It believes the human soul to be a purified form of matter, and that it may become immortal only by physical discipline.

I shall not attempt to discuss these systems of religion in a philosophical or theological manner, but will simply give a sketch of their authors and a brief outline of their teachings.

The author of the first system was *Koong-fu-tsz*, or as Latinized by the Jesuits, *Confucius*. He was born in the small kingdom of Loo, now a part of the Shan-tung province in China, some time about B.C. 550. He was therefore contemporary with Pythagoras, lived a hundred years earlier than Socrates, and a hundred years later than Buddha. His ancestors for generations had enjoyed ducal honors, and his immediate family boasted some of the most illustrious names on the military register of their times. His father, *Heigh*, was distinguished as a cavalry officer of great strength and courage. He was also prime minister of his native kingdom. It is said that at the siege of Pihyang the enemy succeeded in entering the city in such numbers that it became necessary for him and his associates to abandon it. As they were passing through the gate the portcullis fell. Heigh seized the massive structure, and by main strength lifted it and held it up until the last one of his men had passed out. Many other extraordinary exhibitions of physical strength are related of this Chinese Goliath. He is said to have been more than eight feet high.

Confucius was, like his father, a man of great physical strength, and of an irascible and imperious temper in his youth; but by self-discipline he subdued the violence of his passions and became quiet and affable in manner, a studious scholar, and a wise counselor. But little is known of his mother. The Chinese do not affect respect for female biography.

Many absurd legends connected with the birth of Confucius are recorded by grave historians. One is that " as his mother, a few days before his birth, passed through the forest, the trees bent down in homage, and the birds made obeisance to her." "He was born in a cave, and a spring of water gushed up at the moment of his birth, in which he was washed, after which the spring dried up. Two dragons watched at the entrance of the cave, one on the right and the other on the left."

The Chinese believe Confucius to have been inspired by heaven, though not himself divine, and therefore regard the appearance of miracles at his birth not incredible. They say their sages are not gods nor related to the gods, but a superior development of man, endowed by heaven with extraordinary mental and moral powers for the enlightenment of mankind. Accustomed as we are to the perspicuity and harmony of truth, the incongruities and absurdities which superstition associates with the supernatural offend our sense of propriety. Mystery—incomprehensibility—is the heathen idea of the divine; and as Confucius was a man of decided human character, and in no sense veiled in mystery, his followers have deified him as a man and placed him at the head of their sages, and not among their gods. It is true they worship him, but so they do the shades of deceased emperors, and their own ancestors, as well as the heroes and benefactors who have been deified by imperial decrees.

The childhood of Confucius was passed as that of most boys of his time. His father left him an orphan in his third year, and with limited means, so that his early opportunities for acquiring an education were not good. At that day there were no public schools in China where he could obtain even the rudiments of a primary education. He was therefore left to the resources of his own genius and industry.

Confucius began very early the study of antiquity. He soon discovered that the teaching of the sages was almost entirely unknown among the rude inhabitants of his native state, and he set himself the task of teaching them. His superior intelligence, devotion to the sages of antiquity, and the exemplary character of his life, inspired veneration for his person and profound respect for his teachings. He soon became conscious of his mission as a reformer, and began in good earnest his life work, which he never perhaps fully understood, impelled, as he once said, " to move forward without foreseeing the end." He attributed the impulse which urged him "to become a public teacher of rectitude " to the " will of heaven." In his twenty-seventh year he began his public career as teacher, and such was the reputation which he had already acquired that his academy was soon crowded with aspiring young men from all parts of the country. The simple and suggestive method which he employed as a teacher tested the zeal and ability of his pupils, and many came to see and hear who had not the courage to remain. He said in regard to his method as a teacher: "I do not open truth to one who is not eager to acquire. I present one angle of a subject to a pupil, and if he cannot find the other, I do not repeat the lesson." His school was evidently no place for idlers or dullards.

After some years of labor as a teacher, he was made prime minister of his native kingdom of Loo, a position which his father had once filled. Chinese historians say that "during his administration all useless ornament was abandoned, strict honesty maintained by all grades and classes, and the palmy and pure days of the sages realized again. The women were taught humility and subordination, the children filial piety, the subjects reverence and obedience to their rulers, and the rulers were enjoined to maintain justice and mercy toward all." These golden days, however, were destined to end abruptly; and the happy inhabitants of Loo, so pure, so upright, such models of virtue, were captivated and led astray by a band of singing women sent into their midst by a wicked and wily prince of a neighboring state, whose jealousy could not brook the marvelous prosperity of Loo. Such was the disgust and humiliation of Confucius at the shameful defection of his people, that he left them and became a stranger and wanderer in other lands. He traveled from one petty kingdom to another, pursuing what would now be regarded as the life of a respectable vagabond, followed in all his eccentric wanderings by a few faithful disciples, whom he taught under the friendly shade of some tree or by the bank of some stream, borrowing from familiar objects in nature the striking imagery which characterized his style as a teacher. Many of the lessons thus taught have been preserved, and now form a part of his philosophical teachings.

How far his views of man as a social and sympathetic being have been affected by his personal experience during these years of hardship, disappointment, and sorrow, has formed a subject of grave and voluminous speculation. Some of the dogmas of his code have been attributed to his peculiar trials during his season of exile. He seems to have been above any feelings of revenge, for after some years spent abroad he returned to his native state, and though he refused to accept office, he used his great influence in support of the government. Chastened and made wiser by the hardships and disappointments of life, his teachings assumed at this time a broader and more philosophic cast, and from this period his genius asserted its supremacy over his countrymen. He felt that neither princes nor people appreciated him, and as he approached the end of life he became melancholy. The world had treated him badly. Few understood him. Disappointed hopes filled his soul with bitterness. No wife nor child stood by him to minister the kindly offices of affection. He offered no prayer, and he betrayed no fears. Darkness came over him like the shadows of night, and his great soul went out alone to meet its Maker.

The system of Confucius is to be found in the nine books which bear his name. An analysis of these books would occupy more space than can here be given. The great work of Dr. Legge, "A Translation of the Chinese Classics, with Critical Notes," in seven volumes, contains the most complete and reliable account of Confucianism that we have in the English language, and to that I would refer anyone wishing further information on the subject.

In any attempt to form a just estimate of the great Chinese sage, and his teachings, the intellectual and moral condition of the country in which he lived and labored must be taken into the count. Contemporary with Pythagoras, he belongs to an age anterior to the birth of modern civilization, before Christianity had shed its light upon the intellectual darkness of the world. China had no established system of philosophy, religion, or politics; nothing beyond the traditions of antiquity, and these greatly obscured by oriental exaggeration. There was no literature, no schools, no colleges, nor any of the appliances so common in civilized countries for the diffusion of general intelligence. It is true that Confucius professed only to restore the lost knowledge of antiquity, but how could he do this when the golden age from which he claimed to have gathered so much had no history?

Confucius probably used the names of the ancient sages to give dignity and authority to what would otherwise have been challenged by his countrymen as unlawful innovations. China has always worshiped the past, and the appearance of novelty has been the sign of heresy. As it was, he suffered persecution from those whose condition he labored to improve, the common lot of good men in a corrupt age—the inheritance of reformers. His persecutions would have been much greater if he had attempted any radical changes in his own name. He therefore protected himself and his teachings by claiming to originate nothing, but simply to restore the ancient system of China —the lost wisdom of the sages.

Most ancient Asiatic systems of philosophy and political economy were founded on the prevalent religious notions of their times. Not so with the teachings of Confucius. So little has religion to do with his system that by many of his own countrymen, as well as by some foreign writers, he is regarded as an atheist. Engaged all his life in politics, he seems to have given no thought to the spiritual nature of man or his future destiny, but to have given all his energies to the improvement of human government. The results of his teaching may be seen in China to-day, both in the peculiar form of civil government and in the social institutions of the country. (See Chapter VII. on the Government of China.)

It will be sufficient, perhaps, to give in this connection a brief summary of the leading principles upon which the system of Confucius is founded, especially his views of government.

1. Government is the regulation of human conduct by just and merciful laws, enforced by the authority of the state; rewarding the obedient and punishing the rebellious.

2. The individual multiplied constitutes the family; the family multiplied constitutes the state.

3. He that can govern himself can govern a family; he that can govern a family can govern a state. All good government therefore begins with self-government.

4. In the regulation of individual conduct five things are requisite: benevolence, rectitude, propriety, wisdom, and truth. These are known as the "five cardinal virtues," the "five pillars which support heaven." These virtues cannot exist without a motive, some all-pervading influence. *This universal support is filial piety.* " Without this," says Confucius, "it is useless to expect fidelity to the prince, affection to brethren, justice to neighbors, kindness to domestics, or constancy among friends. This feeling, if it rule in the heart, will lead to the performance of every duty, the subjugation of every evil passion, and the renovation of the whole man. It is not to be confined to time or place, but it is to be maintained whether the objects be present or absent, living or dead." Thus filial duty is made the center and basis of the entire system of civil and social government.

8

The emperor is the "father of his people," for whom he is supposed to feel a constant paternal solicitude, and over whom he exercises unlimited patriarchal authority. He is, theoretically, responsible only to heaven for his conduct.

Confucius was the author of many moral maxims which have had great influence upon the character and habits of the Chinese. He also meddled with the vagaries of speculative philosophy. All the pagan nations of the East have a more or less elaborate cosmogony to which their sages have devoted much thought to little profit. The Chinese philosophers say that "before heaven and earth were divided there existed one universal chaos. When the two energies of nature, male and female, began to exert their harmonizing influence, the purer elements ascended and formed the material heavens; the grosser descended and formed the earth. From these all things sprang into being, and thus heaven and earth are the father and mother of all things." This sexual system runs through the universe, like that which Linnæus found to exist in plants, and forms the basis of universal classification. They find its type and illustration in numbers. "One produced two, two produced four, four produced eight," and thus the endlessly diversified forms in nature were produced. To such studies Confucius devoted the last days of his life.

The demeanor and habits of Confucius have been diligently recorded by his admirers. One says "he was mild, yet firm; majestic, though not harsh; grave, yet agreeable." He seems to have been fond of a simple and retired life. "The virtues of country people," he observes, "are beautiful: he who in selecting a residence refuses to dwell among them cannot be considered wise." Being asked by a disciple to describe the man of superior virtue, Confucius replied: "He has neither sorrow nor fear." The disciple, surprised, said: "Does that alone constitute his character?" The sage responded: "If a man searches within, and finds nothing wrong, he need have neither sorrow nor fear."

It is not an easy task to ascertain the place which Confucius justly occupies among the great teachers of mankind. If we look only to the intellectual and literary character of his writings, and compare them with the Iliad of Homer, the Dialogues of Plato, or the reasonings of Socrates, we must assign him a secondary position. But if we consider the moral influence his teachings have exerted over so many millions of minds for so many ages, we must allow him to rank with the greatest intellects of the world. In any attempt to form an estimate of his character, we must not forget that he was a heathen, and that his opinions on the subject of religion were formed without any knowledge of revelation, but conformed to the crude and absurd religious systems of his time. He said nothing definitely about a future state of existence, but left his disciples to believe the popular teachings of the priesthood on the subject. When approaching death himself, he seems to have felt no great concern about the future. He had been engaged in politics all his life, had given little or no thought to the subject of religion, and died as he had lived.

BUDDHIST PRIEST.

## CHAPTER X.

### Religions of China (Continued).

#### BUDDHISM.

IN any discussion of Buddhism it is important to remember that there are many systems of belief bearing this name. No other faith has undergone so many changes both of doctrine and of ritualistic forms. Buddhism is one thing in China, and quite another thing in Thibet, Japan, Ceylon, Siam, Burmah, and India. It has been greatly modified in China by the influence of Confucianism, Taoism, and ancestral worship. The widely different opinions which have been expressed as to the teachings of Buddhism may therefore be the result of the various forms which it has assumed. In China it has been forced into coalescence with other systems of belief, under the peculiar form of toleration practiced in that country. The Chinaman really has no religious belief. What seems to be a religion with him is a ceremonial or cult used on state occasions, at funerals, and in ancestral worship. He regards the different systems of religious belief prevalent in his country pretty much as we do insurance companies. He takes out a policy in each, and pays the premiums, with the uncertain feeling that it may or may not be a good investment. If Christianity could come into the business it would largely increase the number of its nominal converts. The Chinese are intensely mercenary.

With this introductory explanation, I will give as fair and full a statement of Buddhism, *as it exists in China*, as my space and material will permit.

Buddhism originated in India about six hundred years before our era. It was introduced into China A.D. 66. The Emperor Ming, of the Han dynasty, heard, in some way, that a divine teacher of great wisdom and marvelous power had appeared in the west, and sent an embassy to make inquiries concerning him. The embassy proceeded to India, and there met with the Buddhists; and convinced that Buddha was the divine teacher referred to, they persuaded a number of Buddhist priests to accompany them to China. They were received with great favor by the emperor. Provision was made for their support, temples erected, and their religion gladly received by the people. Buddhism supplied a want which the masses of the people had long felt: some provision for the spiritual nature of man, and some definite teaching as to a future state of rewards and punishments. The old religions of China said nothing about a future life. Buddhism, on the contrary, teaches the existence of the soul after death, and a state of rewards and punishments in a heaven and in a hell. Imperfect and unsatisfactory as this teaching is, it is infinitely better than the cold, heartless teaching of the Confucian system, or the coarse meterialism of Taoism. Buddhism has always been the most popular religion in China with the common people, though held in comparative contempt by the government and the literary classes.

The founder of Buddhism was a son of the king of Magadha, in Bahar, India. Tradition represents him as being in early life grossly dissipated and immoral, but he reformed and devoted himself to a life of separation from the world, and was therefore accounted very holy. He is regarded by his worshipers as one of the manifestations—the last avatar—of Vishnu, and therefore the real Buddha. During his life he was known as "the lion," or devotee of the race of Sakya, and after his death as Buddha, and has been worshiped as such down to the present day.

Buddhism contains less that is revolting and immoral than any other heathen system known in the East except Confucianism. Its influence in China has been to some extent beneficent, chiefly from the fact that it regards man as responsible for the moral quality of his actions. It also inculcates purity, charity, and benevolence.

The principal precepts of Buddhism are ten. They are the following: (1) "Thou shalt not kill." This refers to all creatures that have life, whether man or beast or insect. Life with a devout Buddhist is sacred, no matter in what form it manifests itself. The doctrine of the transmigration of souls adds emphasis to the first commandment, because we cannot know what soul may be incarnate in the creature we would slay. It would be an awful crime to thus destroy a father or mother, and so the commandment covers all forms of life. (2) "Thou shalt not steal." (3) "Thou shalt not commit adultery." (4) "Thou shalt not lie." (5) "Thou shalt not slander." (6) "Thou shalt not desire the death of thine enemies." (7) "Thou shalt not covet." (8) "Thou shalt abhor all idle and indecent conversation." (9) "Thou shalt not betray the secret of another." (10) "Do not err in the true faith, or think it false."

Those who would attain higher degrees of holiness must also obey the following commandments: "Thou shalt not marry, drink intoxicating liquors, smell odoriferous flowers, wear costly garments, or eat food in the afternoon." * Where can we find a better code of laws governing the individual or social life, except in our own inspired Scriptures, where we have "the perfect laws?" There is in our "Ten Commandments" a complete system of moral law without a weak word, or an imperfect phrase, or anything approaching the absurd or unreasonable. Not so with the precepts of Buddha. What reason can be given for the prohibition against smelling "odoriferous flowers," or "eating food in the afternoon?" It is true, smelling the flowers might be considered a luxury, and therefore forbidden; and eating in the afternoon a sign of gluttony, and so condemned as a sin, but what trifles compared with the many

---

\* These commandments apply chiefly to the priesthood.

things not prohibited! There is nothing of this kind of frivolity in our Scriptures.

Buddhism has no Saviour, no atonement, but leaves the sinner to deal with himself in a business way. He is supposed to open a debit and credit account with himself and heaven. If at the end of life his good deeds overbalance his evil deeds, then he is entitled to reward, and will enjoy in the future state whatever good may be reserved for the righteous. If, on the other hand, his evil deeds preponderate, he will be doomed to suffering according to the demerit of his sins.

One way of laying up merit is to repeat the name of Buddha. This may be carried to any extent the devotee is able to repeat the sacred name. When a person has repeated it three hundred thousand times, he may begin to hope for a vision of the god. Another method of laying up treasure in heaven is to enter a small cell and have the entrance sealed so that the devotee cannot get out until the end of the time for which he has taken a vow, usually three or five years. His sole occupation is repeating the name of Buddha. He uses a rosary like the Roman Catholics. Many lose their reason while incarcerated in their narrow cells, and are regarded as inspired persons ever afterwards.

Besides the repetition of prayers to Buddha, there are other means of acquiring merit, such as repairing a road, building a bridge, giving ground for a grave, giving alms to the poor. All these acts are esteemed meritorious, and the man who performs them is accounted righteous. The highest rewards are given to those who make an image of Buddha, or write a sermon on his doctrine, or perform any act which may benefit a priest, such as giving him money, building or decorating a temple, etc.

Absorption is considered the highest state of bliss which any mortal can attain; to be swallowed up in " the eternal essence "—a state of utter unconsciousness in which personality is lost. It is annihilation. But few, however, reach this sublime state of absolute rest. It requires a life of peculiar sanctity, many repetitions of the name of Buddha, and many acts of mercy and charity; also perfect abstraction from the world in which the pleasures of sense no longer allure the passions or disturb the tranquil repose of the spirit. If a man can become so holy as to stop thinking entirely, he may be sure of happiness when he dies. It is pathetic to see a poor blind soul thus struggling after the light: burdened with a sense of sin, oppressed with the cares and anxieties of life, wandering to and fro, seeking rest and finding none. Surely the great Father of us all regards with tender compassion these lost sheep of the wilderness.

### THE TRANSMIGRATION OF SOULS.

This is one of the principal dogmas of Buddhism, and one of the most universal tenets in heathenism. The end of all the weary changes through which the soul must pass in its transmigrations is annihilation, or to "be swallowed up in the crystal sea of universal being." All the devotees of Buddhism do not expect this highest estate, or if they do hope for it they must expect to toil through the changes of the "thirty-three heavens." This will require ages upon ages. The soul, when it enters the spirit world, is judged and sent on its endless round of transmigrations, either up or down in the scale of existence. The man who has lived a wicked and unclean life in this world will descend and perhaps enter the body of some beast or worm, to grovel in the dust among the lowest forms of animal life. In some remote period, when he has atoned for his sins by suffering, he may return to this world again and be born a man or a horse, an ox or a woman.

The idea upon which the doctrine of transmigration is based seems to be connected with the Buddhist theory of the creation. The Buddhists believe that matter is eternal, and that anything which has life has within itself that which has brought it into existence, and also contains within itself a certain tendency to a fixed destiny. The world was brought into existence by this law of tendency, and it is destined to destruction, to be followed by another world, and that by another, and that by myriads of other worlds. The period of the world's existence is called a kalpa. One writer has said, in trying to illustrate the duration of a kalpa: "If a man were to walk up a mountain nine miles high once in every hundred years, and continue to do so until the mountain was worn down to a plain, the time required would be nothing compared with the fourth part of a kalpa." Now, as one world when destroyed springs up again to pass through another stage of existence, so man when he dies merely passes into another state of being, to come into the world again at some future time. What his condition shall be depends upon his conduct in the previous state of existence; what kind of an animal he will be, how long he will continue, etc., will depend upon his character.

A very wicked man may pass at once into hell when he dies. He will thus be deprived of the opportunity to repent, or to acquire merit by good deeds. According to the sacred books of the Buddhists there are eight principal and sixteen smaller hells. They are inclosed on all sides by high walls thirty-six miles thick. All kinds, all conceivable modes of torture are inflicted on the wicked in these hells. In one place a man is being pounded by a large hammer until his bones are crushed to a jelly. Another is having the flesh torn from his bones with red-hot pinchers. Some are roasted on spits, some have melted lead poured down their throats, and others are boiled in oil. The man who has murdered his father or mother suffers all the torments of all the hells forever.

The Buddhist heaven (or heavens, for there are thirty-three in all) is a place of rest and perfect enjoyment, where the inhabitants are exempt from toil and sorrow, from sickness and suffering. They dwell in beautiful palaces, and spend their time in dancing with beautiful goddesses. This lovely place is sometimes called "The Happy Land in the West." It is a country of gardens and palaces, with birds of melodious song, and where all desires are fully gratified. This state of blessedness can be attained only by the most enthusiastic devotees of Buddha, after long ages of toil and suffering, in which an infinite amount of merit has been acquired.

Such is a brief outline of the Buddhist creed, so far as it exists among the common people in China. There is a metaphysical phase of Buddhist teaching which belongs rather to philosophy than religion. With this the Chinese have little sympathy. They are practical, not speculative. This "higher Buddhism," as it is called, has captivated the imaginations of some Europeans who affect much admiration for its "lofty and sublime character." This is what Sir Edwin Arnold calls "The Light of Asia." It is poor philosophy, and worse religion. His poem is beautiful enough, but it is poetry, not a fair account of Buddhism, not even an imitation of it, as it actually exists in China.

The dogma of transmigration is degrading to man in every feature of it. It places him on a level with the beasts that perish, and in its practical workings sinks him far below the irrational creation, even to the vilest and most disgusting forms of life. To-day he is a man with reason, affections, hopes, fears, joys, and sorrows; to-morrow he is a whining dog, the companion of owls and bats, or a wild beast of the jungle; to-day he may command an army or rule a nation; to-morrow he may be chased by the hunter's hounds!

An old man in China once said to a missionary: "I have for some time past lived on the emperor's benevolence. The priests assure me that after death I shall be obliged to repay the emperor's generosity by becoming a post horse to carry his dispatches. They exhort me to take care not to stumble, or wince, or bite. They tell me if I travel well, eat little, and am patient, I may excite the compassion of the gods, and be born into the world as a man of rank. Sometimes I dream that I am ready harnessed for the rider, and I wake in a sweat, hardly knowing whether I am a man or a horse. They tell me that people of your religion continue to be men in the next world as they are in this. I am ready to embrace your religion, for I had rather be a Christian than become a beast." He was baptized and died happy, believing that he was saved from being a post horse.

Buddhist priests are seen everywhere in China. They have little influence personally with the people. They are regarded as mere servants whose business it is to take care of the temples, idols, and the furniture belonging to the temples. They are, as a rule, ignorant of everything except the manual service required of them, and such professional attention at funerals, feasts, etc., as custom demands. The literary class denounces them as an ignorant, idle, and lazy set, and the people generally despise them, except when acting in their office as priests. Not only are they idle and lazy, but they are grossly immoral, spending their time in gambling and smoking opium. Their numbers are recruited from the lower ranks of society, especially from the very poor families.

I have thus sketched Buddhism as it exists in China. It is that form of Buddhism which the Chinese accept—the popular form—and not Buddhism as it exists in India. The Buddhism of India bears somewhat the relation to Brahmanism that Protestantism does to Romanism.* The Brahmans persecuted the Buddhists of India with great cruelty, and this caused the Buddhist priests to become missionaries and spread their religion through other countries. They are in China, Tartary, Thibet, Siam, Japan, Ceylon, and other countries of the East. Buddhism is the best heathen religion in the world. It has been called "The Christianity of the East." This is a little too much praise. It does not approach our blessed Christianity, except remotely in its benevolent teachings. There is but one "name under heaven given among men whereby we must be saved"—the name of Jesus Christ.

---

*The Buddhists were reformers.

TEMPLE OF THE FIVE HUNDRED GODS.

## CHAPTER XI.

### RELIGIONS OF CHINA (CONTINUED).

#### TAOISM.

TAOISM is the least influential system of religious belief in China. It is too mystical for the practical Chinese. Its founder, Lau-tsz, was a contemporary of Confucius, and the two once met. Confucius said he could not understand Lau-tsz, and never afterwards sought any intercourse with him. His only book that has survived the ages is a work entitled "Reason and Virtue," an exceedingly obscure production, both in style and sentiment.

Many foolish stories are told of Lau-tsz, such as that he was eighty years old when born; that he had appeared on earth three different times at intervals of a thousand years; and other absurd legends. He spent his life as an ascetic in solitude, and taught that man's spiritual nature can best be purified, and his passions brought under control, by habitual silence and meditation.

It is impossible to give an intelligent expression to what we do not understand. The vagaries of Taoism are utterly incomprehensible to a Western mind. For example, the existence of the world is thus accounted for: "Reason produced one, one produced two, and two produced three, and three produced all things." Again: "Before the birth of heaven and earth, there existed only an immense silence in illimitable space; an immeasurable void in endless silence." No wonder Confucius said he could not understand Lau-tsz! The reader is probably in the same mental condition as to the meaning of the above extract. I could add many more specimens of the same lucid character, but presume enough has been given to satisfy even the most curious.

The forms of worship and other religious rites of the Taoists resemble those of the Buddhists so nearly that the differences are discernible only in the dress and general appearance of the priests of the two sects. The Buddhists shave off all the hair of their head, while the Taoists leave a tuft of hair on the back of the head. The official robes of the Taoists are not so long as those of the Buddhist priests. Those of the Buddhists are yellow, and those of the Taoists are red.

The Taoists profess to have great power over evil spirits—" the demons of the invisible world." The high priest, or head of the sect, like the Lama of Thibet, is supposed to be immortal; that is, as soon as one dies another is appointed to take his place, and the spirit of the dead priest enters into his successor. Thus the office is perpetual, while the individual is, like other men, mortal.

Dr. Medhurst, in his " State and Prospects of China," mentions some curious ceremonies observed by the Taoists. He says: "Death is with them peculiarly unclean, and whenever it occurs brings a number of evil influences into the dwelling, which are only to be expelled by the sacrifices and prayers of Taoist priests. This is what they call 'cleansing the house;' and as it is attended by some expense, many prefer turning lodgers and strangers out in dying circumstances rather than have the house haunted with ghosts for years afterwards." They also have a ceremony for cleansing districts from contagion. "One of the solemnities is celebrated on the third day of the third moon, when the votaries of Taoism go barefoot over lighted charcoal, by which they fancy that they triumph over the demons they dread, and please the gods they adore. On the anniversary of the birth of the 'high emperor of the somber heavens' they assemble before the temple of this imaginary being, and having made a great fire, fifteen or twenty feet in diameter, they go over it barefooted, bearing the gods in their arms." They chant prayers, ring bells, sprinkle holy water, blow horns, brandish swords with which they strike the fire, to subdue or frighten away the demons. Other ceremonies of the Taoists will be described hereafter.

### TEMPLES, FORMS OF WORSHIP, ETC.

It will be appropriate to close the chapters on the "Religions of China" with some account of the temples and temple worship of the Chinese.

The most conspicuous buildings in a Chinese landscape are the temples, pagodas, and the offices of the government officials. The temples dedicated to Buddha, the pagodas and shrines connected with this sect, far outnumber all the others put together. All are built after the same model, though differing greatly in size and expensiveness. Some cost hundreds of thousands of dollars, others a few thousand, and some only a few hundred. It is considered a very meritorious act to aid in building a temple or pagoda. Some wealthy men build temples at their own expense, as rich men sometimes build churches in Christian countries.

Temples dedicated to the worship of Confucius exist in every district and in every department of the empire, where ceremonies in honor of the great sage are performed by the mandarins in the second and eighth months of every year. These temples differ from the Buddhist temples in many respects. Externally they present nothing very striking, but within they are richly ornamented. The floor is paved with stone slabs. The roof is supported by immense columns, and the woodwork near the roof is covered with landscape paintings in the best style of Chinese art. There is no ceiling. There are no images, except perhaps a statue or painting intended to represent the person of Confucius; but it is not worshiped. The "spirit tablets" stand for the sage and his most distinguished disciples. These "tablets" are nothing but small pieces of board, neatly varnished, and each inscribed with the name of one of the sages. They are inserted into little pedestals, so as to make them stand upright in their places.

The offerings presented to Confucius consist of animals, silks, wine, and vegetables. It is estimated that there are about fifteen hundred temples dedicated to Confucius in the Chinese empire, and that there are annually offered to him sixty-two thousand pigs, rabbits, sheep, and deer, and twenty-seven thousand pieces of silk. These offerings are presented very early in the morning, usually before daylight. Spectators are not permitted to be present, and no priest is allowed to have any part in the service. Occasionally a foreigner manages to witness, in a clandestine way, these strange rites. An American thus describes what he witnessed on one occasion in the Confucian temple at Shanghai: "In front of the great tablet of Confucius, and a little to the right, we saw the carcass of a large ox, the skin having been removed, placed on a rack, its head facing the altar. On the left a pig and a goat were placed in a similar position. A pig and a goat were also placed before the tablets of the seventy-two disciples, and a piece of carpeting on the floor indicating where the worshipers were to kneel. The altar is nothing but a long table painted red. The principal officer entered the hall, preceded by two musicians, one tapping a small drum, the other playing a flute. He stopped in front of the door in the court. An attendant cried out to him in a loud voice, and he dropped on his knees. Then the word is given to "knock head," and the worshiper strikes the ground three times with his head, and then rises to his feet. This ceremony is repeated three times. The worshiper then enters the great hall and kneels before the tablet of Confucius, an attendant kneeling on his right, and another on his left. A third attendant takes a small box from the altar and hands it to the attendant kneeling on the left, and he passes it to the worshiper. He takes it in both hands, elevates it a moment, and then gives it to the attendant kneeling on his right, who places it on the altar. This ceremony is repeated before each tablet in the hall."

The foregoing is only a part of the tedious, and to a stranger meaningless, ceremony. I have given thus much as a sample of the whole two hours' performance, enough I presume to afford the reader some idea of the character of the service. The Confucian temples are closed except on the two days of worship in the year, and are not therefore, like the Buddhist temples, places of resort for the common people. I visited one Confucian temple, but witnessed no act of worship.

Buddhist temples are not only numerous in China, but many of them are spacious buildings, furnishing a permanent home for several hundred priests, besides ample room for the many large idols which they contain, and the multitudes of worshipers who throng their halls and altars. During his residence in China the writer visited several large monasteries and many common Buddhist temples. A description of one may serve as a general description of all, for they differ chiefly in size and elaborateness of finish. Some of them are grand and elegant structures, others are neglected and filthy. They are usually situated on some elevation surrounded by natural scenery. Many of the large monasteries cover several acres, and are an ornament to the city and surrounding country.

I have in mind a temple which may be taken as a fair representative of all others. It is situated inside the city walls, and is a popular shrine where multitudes of the common people worship. The main building presents an imposing front. It is open, and the large image of Buddha, which occupies a central position just inside the entrance, is visible from the time you enter the gate of the inclosure. This image is fifteen or twenty feet high, though in a sitting posture. He wears a crown of blue filigree work of curious shape. His throne rests on a square base, so covered with gaudy drapery as to resemble a show stand. In front of him is an altar on which incense is kept burning, and near it a long rack for candles. The image of Buddha does not resemble the Chinese features, but rather the Hindoo. The countenance wears a quiet, benevolent expression, and the whole impression is pleasing. On either side of the entrance stands a guardian. The one on the right hand is an enormous black giant, who grasps a bludgeon in his right hand and a dagger in his left. The one on the opposite side is a more fearful-looking creature, if possible, than the other. He is fully eighteen feet high, and flourishes a thunderbolt in one hand and a flaming torch in the other. Near these monsters stand two assistants, who, though less fierce in countenance, are by no means attractive. Immediately in the rear of the image of Buddha, and separated from it by a thin partition, is another idol. This figure holds in his hand a club with which to beat off the evil spirits that might wish to disturb the services.

In the rear of the front room is another building, sixty feet deep, and perhaps one hundred feet wide. This is devoted to the worship of the "Three Precious Buddhas." Here the priests assemble morning and evening for worship. Against a high gilded screen in the rear are placed the three idols. Their size corresponds to the other images. Their faces are mild and expressive of benevolence. These figures represent the past, present, and future incarnations of Buddha.

The third temple is situated still farther in the rear, and contains several images of the "Goddess of Mercy." The largest of the three images sits in the middle, and the two smaller ones on each side. In time of famine or pestilence prayers are offered to this popular goddess. Her image is sometimes carried through the streets, that all may be able to see and worship it.

There are other buildings connected with the main temple, in which the priests reside, and for other purposes. There are also libraries belonging to the monasteries and larger temples. In all the rooms of the main building there are idols with altars in front of them on which incense is burned, and mats on the floor for kneeling worshipers. All the buildings are dark and gloomy, and the associations are not calculated to relieve the somber impression made upon the mind of the Christian visitor.

The reader who has never been in a heathen temple, and who has never witnessed heathen worship, may be interested in a description of a Buddhist service. Dr. Culbertson describes what he witnessed in the island of Poo-to, famous in the annals of Buddhism for the last thousand years. As he entered one of the temples he heard " a low, monotonous chant. The priests were at their devotions. In the elevated shrine sit the Three Precious Buddhas—huge idols, once gaudily gilded and painted, but now dingy with age. The smoke of incense rises from the huge censer which stands upon the altar. In front of the altar stand fourteen priests, erect, motionless, with clasped hands and downcast eyes, a posture which, with their shaven heads and long flowing robes, gives them an appearance of the deepest solemnity. The low and solemn tones of the slowly moving chant they are singing might, but for the hideous idols, awaken solemn emotions. The priests keep time with the music, one by beating on an immense drum suspended from the roof, another on a large iron vessel, and the third on a hollow wooden sounding-piece about the size and shape of a human skull.

Continuing the chant for a short time, they suddenly, at a signal from a small bell in the hand of their leader, kneel upon low stools covered with straw matting, at the same time bowing low and striking their foreheads against the stone pavement. Then slowly rising, they face inward toward the altar, seven facing to the right and seven to the left, and resume their chant. At first they sing in a slowly moving measure, then gradually increase the rapidity of the music until they utter the words as fast as it is possible to articulate, after which they return gradually to the slow and solemn measure with which they commenced. Again a signal from the little bell changes their movement, and they march slowly in procession around the shrine, while one of their number takes a cup of holy water and pours it upon a low stone pillar at the temple door. Thus they continue their prostrations and chanting and tinkling of bells for half an hour or more. This is a fair specimen of the regular worship of the temples."

Some of the priests in a monastery rise long before daylight, and strike their drums and bells to rouse their gods from sleep. Again in the forenoon they are at their devotions, and in the afternoon before sunset they are summoned to vespers. Some of the more devout repeat the morning service after nine o'clock at night. Besides these daily services they are often employed to perform special services for the benefit of some living or dead person, for which they are paid.

Occasionally you will see a priest going through the service in a reverent and solemn manner, but usually they appear utterly indifferent to what they are doing. The prayers and songs they repeat are in the Pali or Sanskrit language, and wholly unintelligible to themselves. The entire ritual is without meaning to priests and people alike.

The people worship in the temples in a solitary manner, there being no social worship, except among the priests, as just described. The common people burn incense, make offerings, and pray to some god for help in trouble, for success in business, or for some special benefit. They often exhibit great earnestness in their devotions. The women do most of the worshiping in the temples. The Goddess of Mercy is their favorite deity. Her shrine is covered with votive offerings. A few nunneries exist under the patronage of the Goddess of Mercy, or Queen of Heaven, as she is sometimes called. The nuns are recruited, like the priesthood, by purchase, or by self-consecration. They are required to live a life of devotion and mortification, eat vegetables, care nothing for the world, and keep themselves busy with the services of the temple, attend the sick, and perform acts of charity. The reader has no doubt already perceived the similarity between the rites of the Buddhists and the Romish Church. Some of the early Romish priests and missionaries believed that these rites had been derived from the Romanists or Syrians who entered China as missionaries before the twelfth century; others referred them to St. Thomas, and some to the devil, who had thus imitated the Roman Catholic Church in order to scandalize Christianity. There is certainly a striking similarity between the Buddhist and Catholic forms of worship, priestly dresses, burning of incense, candles, chants, rosaries, prayers for the dead, etc. Buddhism is older, by six hundred years, than the Roman Catholic Church. Which has most likely copied the other? If one has taken nothing from the other, the points of resemblance between them indicate a marvelous coincidence.

To one brought up in a Christian land, accustomed to the simple forms of divine service, reading the word of God, singing the sweet songs of Zion, hearing the story of God's love for the world, of Christ's beautiful life, his death on the cross, his resurrection, his ascension to heaven, and all the wonders of his miracles and ministry, together with the "communion of saints" and the delightful associations of the house of God—to one thus educated, it is extremely painful to witness the gloomy and unintelligible mummeries of heathen worship. The temples are filled with the images of idolatry, and all connected with the service is not only strange and unmeaning, but depressing and sad beyond expression. There is nothing cheerful or hopeful in it. "Without God, and without hope in the world," those who visit the polluted shrines of idolatry find no comfort for their weary and heavy-laden souls, but return to their homes still bearing their burdens. The mysteries of life perplex them, and the shadow of death fills their anxious souls with gloomy apprehensions. Thus living and dying they are unhappy.

ANCESTRAL HALL.

## CHAPTER XII.

### Worship of Ancestors.

BEFORE saying anything specially about the worship of ancestors, I will notice some of the popular superstitions connected with death. The Chinese seem utterly indifferent to the mere fact of death, or even of what may follow it. This is the result partly of temperament, but chiefly, I think, because they are fatalists. They do not believe that it is possible for anyone to die "until his time comes," and then no power on earth can prevent it. As they believe that a man's future destiny depends on the amount of merit he has acquired, they expect no pardon of sin or commutation of punishment, and therefore accept stolidly the doom which awaits them. Some show signs of fear on the approach of death, but it seems to be only the fear which all animals feel in the conscious presence of danger, or the apprehension of suffering, and not from any sense of sin and the punishment due to it.

The superstitions connected with the death of a person vary in different parts of the country. In some places a piece of silver is put in the mouth of the dying. The nose and ears are also carefully covered, and when death actually takes place a hole is made in the roof of the house to facilitate the exit of the spirits issuing from the body. The Chinese believe a man has six animal spirits, which die with the body, and three souls, one of which enters hades and receives judgment, one remains with the tablets in the ancestral hall, and the third dwells with the body in the tomb. Those who are sent to hell pass through every form of suffering, inflicted upon them by hideous monsters, and are at last released to wander about as homeless demons to torment mankind, or vex themselves in the bodies of animals or reptiles. The priests are employed to pray for those who are supposed to be sent to hell, and after a service, longer or shorter, according to the sum of money paid, the priest declares the soul has crossed the bridge leading out of hell, and is entitled to a letter of recommendation from the priests to the powers who rule in the western heaven. With this letter in hand, the soul is supposed to be kindly received into heaven, or sent to some other good place. This is one form of the superstition. There are many others, absurd, contradictory, and so exceedingly coarse and cruel that I forbear to record them. We are not responsible for the incongruities and absurdities so apparent in these lines. Nothing is more confused and contradictory than superstition; nothing more irrational.

The body is prepared for burial soon after death. It is arrayed in the best dress the family can afford. A fan is put in one hand, and a prayer on a piece of paper in the other. The coffin resembles a section of the trunk of a tree, being made of boards three or four inches thick, and rounded on the outside. When the body is placed in the coffin it is usually covered with quicklime, and the coffin hermetically sealed. Coffins containing the bodies of parents, and other members of the family, are sometimes kept in the house for many years, and incense is burned before them morning and evening. The coffin is sometimes attached by creditors to enforce payment of debt.*

Burial places are located by geomancers with much ceremony, if the family of the deceased be rich. It is important that the *fung shwai*—that is, the "wind and water"—be settled with great care, for if these be not right the soul that dwells with the body in the grave will be very unhappy. If the family be poor, the dead member must be satisfied with any locality, whether lucky or unlucky, which is obtainable. In some instances a space on the surface of the ground the size of the coffin is rented and the coffin placed upon it, with no protection from the weather. I have seen about Shanghai the coffin supported on small stakes two or three feet from the ground, and the soil under it cultivated, thus making the small spot of earth serve a double purpose—feed the living and rest the dead.

When the day of burial arrives, which is usually

---

* Instances are on record of filial sons who have sold themselves into slavery in order to raise money to release the coffin of their fathers.

the first lucky day after death, the friends of the deceased assemble at the house. A band of musicians attends the solemn procession from the home to the grave; the tablet of the departed is carried in a separate sedan chair; the mourners are dressed entirely in white, and the family with wailings and lamentations, assisted by hired mourners, march slowly to the place of interment. When they reach the grave crackers are fired, libations are poured out, and prayers recited by the priests; papers are cut into the shape of money, clothes, and whatever the dead may need in the spirit land. Paper money is also freely scattered around the grave to purchase the good will of any wandering spirits that may be prowling about, and who might disturb or assault the deceased.

The season of mourning for a father is three years, but may be reduced to twenty-seven months. Heavy penalties are inflicted upon those who try to conceal the death of a parent or neglect to observe the rites. For thirty days after a death the nearest kindred must not shave their heads nor change their dress. The best expression of sorrow is supposed to be given in a careless dress and slovenly manner, as if the mourner were so absorbed with grief as to be indifferent to everything else. Half mourning is blue. It is usually indicated by a pair of blue shoes, or a blue cord woven into the hair. The rich often make costly displays of their mourning dresses. The poor simply do the best they can to follow the fashion, and frequently involve themselves in debt that they may make a show. There is nothing in a Chinese funeral that suggests hope. All is gloom. The whole story is told in the pathetic lament of Job: "Man dieth, and wasteth away: yea, man giveth up the ghost, and where is he?"

Funeral ceremonies, like other customs in China, vary somewhat with the locality. I have given what I have witnessed myself in eastern China, and what I understand to be common throughout the empire, with slight modifications.

---

Now that the funeral rites have been properly observed, and the deceased is supposed to be satisfied with all that has been done, the tablet containing the name of the person, the date of his death, etc., is placed in the ancestral hall, where it receives the worship of the living members of the family, along with the other dead kindred. In some households incense is burned before the tablets morning and evening—a sort of family worship. In most families incense and prostrations are presented only at certain seasons of the year.

The great festival connected with the worship of the dead, called "*Ching Ming*," occurs annually about the first week in April, and is observed by all, from the emperor down to the street beggars. The whole population, men, women, and children, repair to the family tombs, carrying their sacrifices, libations, candles, paper, incense, etc., for offerings, and there, in a solemn and decorous manner, perform the rites, prayers, etc., prescribed by custom. The grave is carefully repaired and swept, and at the close of the services signals are left to show that the accustomed rites have been performed. Until a grave is three years old the women are expected to attend along with the men, but after that they are excused.

A table is placed before the tomb, on which are laid the articles to be used in the ceremony—food, incense, and candles. A sacrifice is first offered to the earth, a portion of which is thrown out to the four points of the compass, for the benefit of any wandering ghosts from the neighboring tombs who may happen to be near. In return for this polite attention they are expected to keep off and not disturb the ancestral spirits at their meal. This done, the eldest of the family bows before the table, and is followed in order by the younger worshipers. The following prayer is offered at the tomb by the more intelligent and devout worshipers:

"I, Lin Yu, the second son of the third generation, presume to come before the grave of my ancestor, Lin Kung. Revolving years have brought again the season of spring. Cherishing sentiments of veneration, I look up and sweep your tomb. Prostrate I pray that you will come and be present; and that you will grant to your posterity that they be prosperous and illustrious; at this genial season of showers and gentle breezes, I desire to recompense the root of my existence, and exert myself sincerely. Always grant your safe protection. My trust is in your divine spirit. Reverently I present the fivefold sacrifice of a pig, a fowl, a duck, a goose, and a fish; also, an offering of five plates of fruit, with libations of spirituous liquors, earnestly entreating that you will come and view them. With the most attentive respect, this annunciation is presented on high."

After the prayer, paper money, paper clothes, and other articles are sent off through the flames to the spirit world. Sometimes the money is inclosed in a large envelope, on which is inscribed the name of the person for whom it is intended. After this, long strips of white paper, cut so as to represent strings of copper cash, are tied to a stick, which is stuck in the earth on top of the tomb, and left fluttering in the breeze, an evidence to all, the living and the dead, that the duties of filial piety have not been neglected. This paper money is a cheap way of furnishing supplies to the spirits in the other world. Ten cents' worth of gilt paper is sufficient to furnish a deceased father with all he can use, living in the most luxurious style, for twelve months. Exchange is thus greatly to the advantage of the Chinese in their transactions with their dead ancestors in the spirit world.

The universal belief among the Chinese that the repose of the soul in the future state depends materially upon the pious services of their descendants in this world makes them extremely anxious for offspring. In some cases where a man has no son to worship at his tomb he either adopts a boy or makes provision in his will to have the rites performed. Much that is credited to filial affection in the Chinese is as purely selfish as any other feeling of their sordid nature. They look forward to the time when they will be ghosts in hades and dependent for their happiness upon the attention of the living in this world, and therefore wish the rites of ancestral worship to be perpetuated. Besides this, they also believe that if they do not observe the rites for the souls of their ancestors those souls will become malignant spirits and torment them; they will have bad luck in business, sickness in their persons and families. The Chinese have a servile fear of spirits.

It may be said that most of their religious acts, especially those performed in the temples, are intended to avert misfortune rather than supplicate blessings. In order to ward off malignant influences, amulets are worn and charms hung up by persons of all ranks. Among the latter are money swords made of coins of different sovereigns, strung together in the form of a dagger; leaves of the sweet-flag and Artemisia tied in a bundle. The first is placed near beds, the latter over the lintel, to drive away demons. A man also collects a cash or two from each of his friends, and gets a lock made, which he hangs on his son's neck in order to lock him to life, and make the subscribers surety for his safety. Adult females also wear a neck lock for the same purpose. Old brass mirrors to cure mad people are hung up in the halls of the rich; representations of the unicorn, of gourds, tigers' claws, the eight diagrams, are worn to insure good fortune or ward off sickness. The average Chinese believes that the heavens and the earth are full of evil spirits, and among the most malignant and powerful are the unhappy souls of men—"the lost spirits of bad men."

The worship of ancestors is undoubtedly idolatrous. The dead are worshiped in the same manner and with the same offerings with which the Chinese worship their gods. The prayers addressed to the gods are also offered up before the tablets in the ancestral hall. This superstition is one of the chief hindrances to the spread of the gospel in China.

*DEMONIACAL POSSESSION.*

In addition to what has been said on the subject of "Ancestral Worship" it may be well to give some account of the Chinese belief concerning *demons*. While I was in China, strange stories were told me of demons entering into the bodies of men and women, but I had no opportunity of investigating any case, and was disposed to class this with other foolish superstitions of the people. So far as I know, the missionaries generally held the same views, and no one gave any special attention to the subject until the Rev. John L. Nevius, D.D., of the Presbyterian mission at Chefoo, China, interested by some extraordinary reports brought to him by native Christians, began a serious investigation of the matter. The results of his studies and researches have recently been given to the public in a 12mo volume of 482 pages.

I knew Dr. Nevius (now deceased), and have the utmost confidence in his ability, learning, and strict integrity. He was a careful, conscientious student, painstaking and thorough in his methods, and free from prejudice. What therefore he has said as matter of fact I accept without question, and give great weight to his opinions. He spent forty years in China, and had ample opportunities of thoroughly testing and verifying all the statements he has made concerning the phenomena of this difficult and occult subject.

I shall not undertake to discuss the general subject of demoniacal possessions, but select such facts from Dr. Nevius and others as I suppose will interest the reader. No thoughtful person can fail to see a likeness in the cases here given to the instances of demon possession recorded in the New Testament. I venture to suggest no theory concerning the seeming analogy. The subject is too grave and too difficult for casual treatment, except as a simple narrative of phenomena.

The Chinese discriminate between lunatics and those possessed by demons, both by their appearance and language. The person possessed has a cringing manner, and speaks in the name of the demon, and not in his own. The demoniac sometimes becomes extremely violent, smashes everything near him, exhibits superhuman strength, tears his clothes into rags, and rushes into the street, or into the mountains, or wilderness, unless prevented. After such violent demonstrations he calms down and submits to his fate, but under the most heart-rending protests.

In most cases the demon takes possession of the man's body against his will, and he is helpless. The *kwi*, or demon, has the power of driving out the man's spirit, as in sleep or dreams. When the subject awakes to consciousness he has not the slightest knowledge of what has occurred. The actions of possessed persons vary exceedingly. Some leap about violently, tossing their arms; others are quiet in manner, and only talk wildly, uttering what the demon dictates. The voice is changed—some imitate a bird, some squeal like a pig or bleat like a sheep.

Dr. Nevius summarizes the facts which he has gathered from his own observation, from other missionaries in the field, and from native Christians. In this summary he says:

"Certain physical and mental phenomena, such as have been witnessed in all ages and among all nations, and attributed to possession by demons, are of frequent occurrence in China.

"The person supposed to be possessed by a demon passes into an abnormal state, the character of which varies indefinitely, being marked by depression and melancholy, or even vacancy and stupidity amounting sometimes almost to idiocy; or it may be that he becomes ecstatic, or ferocious and malignant.

"The most striking feature of the cases reported is that the subject represents another personality for the time being, being himself partially or wholly dormant. The new personality presents traits of character utterly different from those which really belong to the subject in his natural state.

"Many persons while possessed give evidence of knowledge which cannot be accounted for. They often appear to know of the Lord Jesus Christ as a divine person, and show an aversion to and fear of him.

"There are often heard in connection with demon possessions rappings and noises where physical cause for them cannot be found; and tables, chairs, crockery, and the like are moved about without, so far as can be discovered, any application of physical force."

Nearly all the incidents related in Dr. Nevius's book were furnished by native Christians—mostly by native pastors. These cases, however, have been carefully investigated by intelligent missionaries, and no one of them seems to have any doubt of the veracity of the witnesses. The missionaries in China have been very careful and cautious in the matter, confining themselves chiefly to the report of the peculiar phenomena, and venturing no hasty opinions on the subject. They have avoided anything that might lead the native Christians into the belief that they claim the power to "cast out devils." The subject is curious and interesting, and of a nature to require very careful handling.

What I have written is intended simply as information, with no definite opinions of my own, except that I think the facts reported are reliable. The subject presents some features of Chinese character which will sooner or later attract the attention of the scientific world.

In India, Japan, Mongolia, Thibet, and Siam similar instances of what the people believe to be demoniacal possessions frequently occur, and the Buddhist priests are supposed to be able to exorcise the demons by their incantations. Bishop Cardwell, of India, has given much attention to the subject, and has furnished some valuable information in connection with "devil dancing," a form of demoniacal possession. He says:

"The devil dancer is not drunk—he has eschewed arrack; he has not been seized with epilepsy—the sequel shows that. He is not attacked with a fit of hysteria; although, within an hour after he has begun his dancing, half his audience are thoroughly hysterical. He can scarcely be mad, for the minute the dance is over he speaks sanely, and quietly and calmly. What is it, then? You ask him. He simply answers: 'The devil seized me, sir.' You ask the bystanders. They simply answer: 'The devil must have seized him.' What is the most reasonable inference to draw from all this? Of one thing I am assured—the devil dancer never 'shams' excitement. Whether this be devil possession or not, I cannot help remarking that it appears to me that it would certainly have been regarded as such in New Testament times."

The bishop says that during a devil dance in India, the priest leading the exercise, there are "shrieks, vows, imprecations, prayers, and exclamations of thankful praise, blended in one infernal hubbub. Above all rise the ghastly gutteral laughter of the devil dancer and his stentorian howls: 'I am God! I am the only true God!' He cuts and hacks and hews himself, and not very infrequently kills himself then and there. His answers to the queries put to him are generally incoherent. Sometimes he is sullenly silent, and sometimes whilst the blood from his self-inflicted wounds mingles freely with that of his sacrifice, he is most benign, and showers his divine favors of health and prosperity all around him. Hours pass by. The trembling crowd stand rooted to the spot. Suddenly the dancer gives a great bound into the air. When he descends he is motionless. The fiendish look has vanished from his eyes. His demoniacal laughter is still. He speaks to this and to that neighbor quietly and reasonably. He lays aside his garb, washes his face at the nearest rivulet, and walks soberly home, a modest, well-conducted man."

What does this all mean? Is there such a thing as demoniacal possession in the present day; and if it does exist, does it differ materially from the "possessions" of the New Testament record? To this question I suggest no answer.

PRACTICING ARCHERY.

CHINESE SOLDIERS.

## CHAPTER XIII.

### The Sciences in China.

THE Chinese have been close observers of nature, and have thus gathered many valuable facts in nearly every department of natural science; but being totally ignorant of the laws of generalization and classification, they have failed to make much progress beyond the observation of phenomena.

The practical character of the Chinese mind has prompted them to ignore or discredit all speculative and abstract investigation, and to confine themselves almost exclusively to " immediate utility." The first question asked in regard to any newly discovered fact is, " What use is it?" If it does not suggest some advantage in a material way, it is instantly discarded as useless. The constitutional ingenuity and industry of the people have led them to make many valuable discoveries, and to invent many useful contrivances, in every department of practical life. But their discoveries and inventions have been left in a primitive state, little having been done to develop or perfect them. The discovery of the polarity of the magnet has never been applied to any extensive practical purpose. The invention of printing has not been improved since the days of the Sung dynasty, in the twelfth century of our era; and the manufacture of gunpowder, though a Chinese invention, is still in a rude state. So it is with all their knowledge belonging to the arts and sciences generally. A few examples illustrating the foregoing observations may here be given.

1. *The Theory and Practice of Medicine.*—The Chinese are a very superstitious people, yet they do not often use incantations and charms as remedies for disease, but employ physicians. The doctors, however, resort to many strange and foolish practices to increase the efficiency of their nostrums. The dissection of the human body is never attempted even by their boldest and most progressive surgeons. They are therefore utterly ignorant of anatomy and physiology. They seem to have no idea of the distinction between venous and arterial blood, nor between muscles and nerves. Theories in great variety are furnished to account for the nourishment of the body, and the functions of the several organs. The pulse is studied with great care as an index to the condition of the body, and the average doctor examines it with great deliberation and solemnity. He believes there is a distinct and different pulse in every part of the body, and in his examination of the patient feels first the pulse in one arm at the wrist, and at two points between the wrist and the elbow, and in several other parts of the body. In this manner he proceeds to distinguish twenty-four different kinds of pulse.* They have no idea of the circulation of the blood.

---

\* Du Halde, quoted by Davis; Dr. Abel.

The Chinese doctors divide diseases and remedies into two classes, *hot* and *cold*. If there is too much heat in the body, they use purgatives freely; if too much cold, they employ hot medicines—pepper, spices, etc. They also mix astrology with their pathology. Jupiter rules over the liver; Saturn over the stomach; Mars over the heart; Venus over the lungs; and Mercury over the kidneys.

Chinese drug stores contain a great variety of simple medicines, such as gums and minerals. These are sold in small packages, each containing one dose, with instructions as to the use to be made of it. The people sometimes cast lots as to what doctor they shall employ, and also as to what medicine they shall use in cases where a doctor is not deemed necessary. Ginseng is found in all Chinese drug stores, and is extensively used as a medicine. It is supposed to rejuvenate the human system, and is very popular with old persons especially. It grows in the northern parts of Asia, and in America. It is quite an item in the trade of the United States and China.

Dr. Williams says: "The practice of the Chinese is much in advance of their theories." They have learned something from experience, and their practical turn of mind has enabled them to profit by experience, so that they can relieve ordinary "ailments" with some skill. They use many roots and herbs in their practice, such as camphor, myrrh, ginseng, rhubarb, gentian, and a great variety of seeds, leaves, and barks. Scarcely any preparation is considered complete without ginseng. The doctors are fond of using poultices and plasters of all kinds. Pills made of tigers' bones are said to be good for weakness of any kind, especially to inspire natural courage.* The hide, hair, hoofs, horns, and bones of the stag are also made into large pills, which are supposed to impart to the patient the qualities which characterize that animal.

Asiatic cholera has been one of the greatest scourges China has ever suffered. The native physicians can do little or nothing to mitigate its severity. The smallpox is always in China, and multitudes die of it every year. Vaccination has been introduced by foreigners, in the eastern provinces especially, and is now used by the natives to some extent, though, as a rule, they prefer their own practice of inoculation. This is done by inserting a little cotton into the nostrils in which a small quantity of the virus of smallpox has been placed. Fevers are not as common as with us. Asthma is frequently met with. Consumption, agues, cutaneous diseases of all kinds, are seen everywhere, and many loathsome examples are exhibited among the beggars on the streets. China suffers with nearly all the diseases that "flesh is heir to."

The Chinese have many medical works, some

---

* A Chinese proverb says: "There is a medicine for disease, but none for fate."

of which show no little research on the part of the authors. Dr. Williams mentions the fact that there are over five hundred medical treatises in the Chinese language. Many of them, most of them, would be considered by Europeans entirely worthless.

2. *Chinese Astronomy.*—The Chinese confound astronomy with astrology, and record eclipses, comets, etc., only as astrological data. A native writer on astronomy, who studied under Europeans, published in 1820 a work in which he gives the following description of the heavens: "The heavens consist of ten concentric hollow spheres, or envelopes; the first contains the moon's orbit; the second, that of Mercury; those of Venus, the sun, Mars, Jupiter, Saturn, and the twenty-eight constellations, follow in order; the ninth envelopes and binds together the eight interior ones, and revolves daily. The tenth is the abode of the celestial sovereign, the great Ruler, with all the gods and sages, where they enjoy eternal tranquillity." The author further says: "There are two north and two south poles, those of the equator and those of the ecliptic. The poles of the ecliptic regulate all the machinery of the heavenly revolutions, and turn round unceasingly. The poles of the equator are the pivots of the primitive celestial body, and remain permanently unmoved. What are called the two poles, therefore, are not stars, but two immovable points in the north and in the south." *

---

* Murray's China

The five principal planets — Mercury, Venus, Mars, Jupiter, and Saturn — with the earth, rule over the year and its four seasons, and correspond with the kidneys, lungs, heart, liver, and stomach. They are denoted by white, black, green, red, and yellow. Any alterations in the sun announce misfortunes to the state or its head, such as revolts, famines, or the death of the emperor. When the moon waxes red, or turns pale, men should be in awe at the unlucky times thus foretokened. The sun is symbolically represented by a raven surrounded by a circle, and the moon by a rabbit on his hind legs pounding rice in a mortar, or by a toad. There is a legend of a beautiful woman who drank the liquor of immortality and immediately ascended to the moon, where she was transformed into a toad, still to be seen on the face of the lunar disk. All the stars are arranged in constellations, and an emperor rules over them, who resides at the north pole. There is also an heir apparent, with empresses, sons and daughters, in this celestial government. The Great Dipper — called the "Northern Peak" — is worshiped as the residence of the Fates, where the duration of human life and other events are fixed.

The reader will perceive that the Chinese have studied astronomy chiefly for astrological purposes, and that of the science of astronomy proper they really know little or nothing. The missionaries, especially the early Romish missionaries, introduced some knowledge of Western sciences into the Chinese Imperial College, and among other things a knowledge of astronomy. "But even with all the aid they derived from Europeans, the Chinese seem to be unable to advance in this science when left to themselves, and to cling to their superstitions against every evidence," says an accepted authority on the subject. Some remnants of European science still linger in a traditional form among them, but have no practical value.

The entire day is divided by the Chinese into twelve hours, beginning with 11 o'clock P.M., and each one of the hours is named after one of the characters in the zodiac. The native method of measuring time is by what is called a " time stick," a rude candle made of clay and sawdust, on which are "hour marks." "As the candle burns, so time goes." In ancient times clepsydras of various forms were used to measure time. There is one at Canton, or was some years ago. European clocks and watches are now pretty generally used by the better class of Chinese at the commercial ports.

3. *Geography.*—The Chinese are ignorant of the form and divisions of the globe; that is, the uneducated people are. Those who have been taught in mission schools, or educated among foreigners, know better, and these are not included in the above statement; nor have I taken any account of such persons in the preceding pages, for

my purpose is to represent the people of China as a body, having common characteristics, and not those whose views and characters have been modified by contact with our Western civilization.

The average Chinese believes that the earth is an immense plain, square in shape, around which the sun, moon, and stars revolve. Some of their ancient books so teach, and so multitudes of the men they call scholars sincerely believe. Their common maps are not only erroneous, but extremely absurd. They represent China as occupying nearly all the land in the world, while the rest of mankind are left to find homes among the islands that fringe their western border. North and South America, Africa, and Australia are entirely omitted, while England, France, Holland, and Portugal, Germany and India, are arranged on the western side of China in a series of small islands and headlands. The eastern side is similarly garnished with islands representing Japan, Loo-Choo, Formosa, Siam, etc.

The Chinese notions of the inhabitants of the "outside countries" are still more whimsical and silly, if possible. I quote the same authority again: "In some parts of the earth's surface they imagine the inhabitants to be all dwarfs, who tie themselves together in bunches for fear of being carried away by the eagles; in other parts the inhabitants are all women; and in another kingdom all the people have holes in their breasts extending through their bodies, through which they thrust a pole, when carrying one another from place to place."* I repeat, lest some one should misunderstand me, these absurdities are original *Chinese* conceptions, not the modified teachings of foreigners garbled and misrepresented by the Chinese, as is often done. We see every now and then a statement to the effect that the Chinese are as well informed on most subjects as the foreign missionaries who go to China to teach them. This is not true of the Chinese people. It may be true, to some extent, of those who have been educated in English schools and colleges, such as the Anglo-Chinese College at Shanghai, and other schools founded and supported by Christian Churches having missions in that field; but such persons do not represent the average Chinese, nor are they included in the general estimate. They are marked exceptions to the rule.

4. *The Chinese Monetary System.*—The only coin authorized by the government is a small copper piece called *stein* by the natives, and *cash* by the foreigners. It is thin and circular in shape, about three-quarters of an inch in diameter, with a square hole in the middle for convenience in stringing. On one side is the name of the reigning dynasty, and on the other side the words "current money." Mints for coining this "cash" are established in every provincial capital, under the imperial board of revenue. Gold and silver are used by weight as bullion. Spanish and South American dollars

---

* See Williams's "Middle Kingdom," Vol. II., p. 155.

are employed in trade, and their value is generally understood throughout the empire.

Chartered banking companies do not exist, but private banks are common, especially in large towns where the necessities of business demand some sort of exchange convenient and reliable. Paper money was used by the Mongols, but for some reason is now unknown as a medium of circulation. The Mongol emperors of China, by acts of repudiation, destroyed all faith in imperial honesty, and the government has had little credit among the people since. This is probably one reason why paper money is unpopular with the people to-day. Bills of exchange, drawn by one banker on another, are extensively employed in the domestic trade of the empire; also promissory notes, and pawnbroker's tickets. The legal interest allowed on small sums is three per cent. per month, but usually on large sums the rate is from twelve to fifteen per cent. per annum.

5. *Chinese Military Science.*—On this subject I shall say little, because I know but little, and because the Chinese know but little. Their unwarlike reputation has been recently emphasized by the war with Japan, in which they suffered a most disastrous and humiliating defeat. The Mongols, Manchoos, Huns, and Tartars all hold the effeminate " celestials " in profound contempt as soldiers. During the Taiping rebellion I witnessed many skirmishes at Shanghai between the imperial troops and the rebels, and I must say

a more absurd display of braggadocio and cowardice it would be difficult to imagine. The soldiers on both sides were poorly equipped for serious work, and the whole affair was a miserable farce, little more dangerous than an earnest game of football! Yet the Chinese called it war!

The regular army, so called, is said to amount to more than a million of men, but in the recent war with Japan not half that number was employed. Of men China has enough, but of soldiers none. They are a peace-loving people, and have conquered their conquerors by their superior intelligence and force of character, and not by arms. The present rulers of China have become Chinese in everything but name, and so it was with the Mongols and Tartars.

The Chinese arms consist principally of bows and arrows, spears, matchlocks, swords, and cannon of various sizes and lengths, and of *flags*. Every tenth man carries a flag. " Terrible as an army with banners " has a meaning in China. Recently the government has purchased foreign arms, gunboats, men-of-war, and other military equipments; but with these I have nothing to do, for they are not *Chinese*, except in a commercial sense, just as any other article of foreign manufacture purchased by the Chinese is their property.

The officers march in the rear when going into battle, to prevent the soldiers from deserting, and to urge them on! They march in front when retreating before the enemy, in order to show their men the best way of escape! For this statement I cannot vouch, though it is not inconsistent with Chinese character. They are a prudent people, and wisely avoid all unnecessary exposure to danger! A Chinese army looks to Europeans very much like a mob of undrilled louts in petticoats. (See illustration.)

6. The Chinese have some general knowledge of natural history, mineralogy, arithmetic, drawing and painting, music, and other sciences, but like their knowledge of medicine, astronomy, geography, etc., it is extremely limited, and may better be called their ignorance than their knowledge of these things. Of natural history some Chinese scholars have made a careful study, or perhaps I should rather say some shrewd observations. Their country furnishes a vast variety of specimens for study in every department of natural history, especially in botany and zoölogy and ornithology.

The domestic animals in China are not as numerous in proportion to the population as with us, for obvious reasons. The hog is common in all parts of the empire, and its flesh constitutes the principal meat food of the lower classes. The wild boar is found in some of the western provinces, but not in central China. As the Chinese do not use milk and butter, cows are met with only in the vicinity of the ports where foreigners reside. The "water buffalo" is used for agricultural purposes. One species of this singular animal is very small, and is seen chiefly in the south. The buffalo of eastern and northern China is a large, uncomely creature, much above the average cow in size, with horns like a goat. It is fond of the water, and in summer plunges into the canals and pools to escape the flies and mosquitoes. It is a sluggish and very tractable animal, much used for riding and drawing in some parts of the country. Sheep are also raised for meat, not for their wool, as the Chinese do not wear woolen clothing.

Among the many varieties of fowls and birds in China, the gold and silver pheasants are conspicuous. They are splendid specimens of the feathered tribes. It is said that one kind, found in the north of China, has tail feathers six feet long. I have seen in an aviary at Shanghai (Mr. Beale's) two of these magnificent birds, surpassing in splendor of plumage the celebrated birds of paradise. The country abounds in wild fowl of all kinds—geese, ducks, pheasants, partridges, grouse, etc. The limits assigned to this chapter will not permit of further notice of the many interesting specimens belonging to this department of natural history.

CHINESE CARPENTER.

CHINESE BLACKSMITH.

## CHAPTER XIV.

### ARCHITECTURE OF THE CHINESE.

CHINESE architecture, like everything else in that strange country, is unique. The original model was evidently the *tent*, for in all their public and private buildings, from the emperor's palace to the fisherman's hut, the resemblance to this type prevails. There are no indications that any effort has been made to develop this simple model into anything higher, or to erect any grand and imposing buildings after the Hindoo or European style. The type is not only primitive, but the material, as a rule, is inferior, and the workmanship clumsy. The structures are consequently generally of a fragile and unsubstantial character. These remarks do not apply to all the buildings, however, but to the ordinary dwellings of the people, which, of course, constitute the principal part of the architecture in city and country. There are no ancient monuments except, perhaps, a few temples and pagodas. There are no great historic ruins. The Great Wall of China may be an exception to this remark, for it was built B.C. 220, and is—much of it—in ruins. China has nothing, however, to compare with the pyramids of Egypt or the ruins of Babylon. The Chinese have not traveled in other lands, or, if they have, they have kept their eyes shut. Their absurd vanity has led them to despise all other people as uncultivated barbarians. One of their writers thus congratulates himself: "I felicitate myself that I was born in China, and constantly think how different it would have been if I had been born beyond the seas in some remote part of the earth, where the people, far removed from the converting maxims of the ancient kings, and ignorant of the domestic relations, are clothed with the leaves of plants, eat wood, and dwell in the wilderness, and live in the holes of the earth. Though born in the world in such a condition, I should not have been different from the beasts of the field. But now, happily, I have been born in the Middle Kingdom. I have a house to live in; have food and drink, and excellent furniture; felicity is mine." This self-satisfied egotist but voices the common sentiment of his fellow-countrymen. We are the barbarians. How could they expect to learn anything from us? In the matter of architecture they have certainly learned nothing.

The dwelling houses of the Chinese are generally only one story high, with no cellars, basements, or attics. The building materials are bricks, matting, wood, and sifted earth made into a kind of concrete. The roof is made of brick tiling. Where stone is abundant, the foundations of the houses are made of it, and are usually very substantial. In many places, however, as at Shanghai, stone is too expensive for such use, and the houses rest on the soil, the whole structure being supported by a wooden framework, which, like a skeleton, furnishes support and gives shape to the building. The walls are made of bricks filled in between the upright posts, which support the roof of the house. The fronts of the dwelling houses have no openings except the doors, with now and then a small square window glazed with oyster shells. This monotonous front is unrelieved by porticoes, steps, or front yards. The better class of houses have inside the outer or street door a small quadrangle, where company is received.

Although the general arrangement of the dwelling houses is substantially the same, yet climate and other causes require some modifications. In the southern and more temperate parts of the empire no provision is made for warming the houses, but in the colder regions, as at Peking, ranges and braziers are used for the purpose of heating the bedrooms. In the less frigid parts of the country the addition of another garment is made to supply the place of artificial heat. The number of jackets worn indicates the degrees of cold or heat—the common thermometer; so many "jackets cold" means so many degrees. The people use foot-stoves and hand-stoves when the weather is very cold. These stoves are often very handsome. They are kept warm by a preparation of pulverized charcoal, which burns slowly and gives out heat steadily. They are very convenient and comfortable.

The houses of the very poor are, as a rule, dark, dirty, and without floors—utterly comfortless. The whole family often live, eat, and sleep in a single room, with the pigs, dogs, and chickens. The furniture consists, perhaps, of a few broken dishes, a rickety stool or chair, and miserable substitutes for beds—a little straw and a few rags. The homes of the poor are always open to the gaze of the passer-by, and to the intrusion of inquisitive strangers. I have been in many such houses, but only once was I permitted to enter the home of a rich family, and then only as far as the library. I saw only the male members of the family. I cannot therefore describe the interior of that home, for I did not see it. The masonry of the Chinese is showy, but unsubstantial, and when neglected soon falls into ruinous decay. It requires constant repairs, and is therefore expensive. When new it looks rather pretty, but a few seasons wear off the flimsy tinsel, and it looks old and shabby.

Public buildings and business houses necessarily differ in style and arrangement from the dwelling houses. Temples and assembly halls are almost the only public edifices in China, except the government buildings, in which the mandarins have their offices. The assembly halls resemble in general appearance the warehouses, having one large room for public meetings. It is said there are more than a hundred in the city of Canton, and a corresponding number in all the cities of the empire. All the dwelling houses, halls, stores, and shops pay a ground rent to the government, the amount of the tax being regulated by the locality, size, and value of the land occupied.

Taverns are numerous, but do not compare with our Western hotels in size or accommodations. They are caravansaries rather than inns or hotels, places where the traveler, who carries his own bedding and provision, may spend a night. Boarding houses, as they exist in Western cities, are unknown in China. Grog shops, gin palaces, or saloons, distinct from the restaurant, do not exist. The Chinese drink " wine," a liquor distilled from rice. It is taken at meals, and is always swallowed hot, like our preparation of coffee and tea. The Chinese moralists have always condemned winedrinking as a vice, and drunkenness is not common among any class. Opium-smoking is the national form of intemperance, and opium shops are as common in China as drinking saloons are in our country. "Tea shops," where at any time, for a few mills, you can get a cup of the refreshing beverage, exist in all parts of the city and country, and are always thronged.

No picture of a Chinese landscape is complete without one or more *pagodas*. These are so familiar to the eye of the reader, as represented in our geographies, that a description is unnecessary. They are connected with Buddhism, and according to the superstitions of that sect bring good luck to the city and surrounding country as far as they can be seen. They are therefore usually placed on some elevation, the higher the better, and so protect a large radius. They are strongly built, and are the only architectural monuments of any great antiquity in China. The word *pagoda* is a word brought from India, and originally meant a temple, but it is used by foreigners to designate the Chinese tower. The native word for pagoda in China is *tah*. It is not a temple, but, as above stated, is intended in some way to promote good luck. It is an ornament to the landscape, whatever else it may be. The great porcelain tower, or pagoda, at Nanking, destroyed by the Taiping insurgents in 1855, was one of the most unique and beautiful structures in the world.

The Chinese have built many bridges across rivers, lakes, and mountain gorges, but my limits will permit only a mention of the fact. There is a bridge of ninety arches near Hangchow. I remember to have seen one of fifty-three arches. The Chinese built suspension bridges at an early day, long before one had been erected in the West. They are said to be the first people to use iron in the construction of bridges.

The Chinese have made little improvement in the art of military fortifications for centuries, and are therefore very far behind the times, as the recent war with Japan abundantly demonstrated. China has probably learned some things concerning the arts of modern warfare during the last few months. She has certainly paid well for the lesson, whether she profits by it or not.

## CHAPTER XV.

### The Dress of the Chinese.

THE full dress of the Chinese, both of the men and women, when you have once become accustomed to it, is not displeasing. It is in a general way commodious and graceful, warm in the winter and reasonably cool in the summer. The shaven crown of the men, with the long braided cue, and the cramped feet of the women, always offend the taste of Western people. They are essentially ugly, for they are unnatural deformities. The Chinese, however, affect to admire them, notwithstanding they are really badges of inferiority; the cue being the sign of political subjugation, and the cramped feet of the women a sign of their social and domestic servitude. In this, "they glory in their shame."

Fashions in dress exist in China as in our own country, but they do not change so often. The general style of the present time has not changed for centuries, and garments of fur or silk are handed down for generations, never being abandoned because out of fashion. I once had a teacher in China who wore, with pride, an outer garment which belonged to his grandfather. The teacher was then himself an old man, and his son was looking forward to the time when the ancient tunic would become his property, and perhaps descend to his grandson. The fabrics most worn by the Chinese are silk, cotton, and linen for summer, with the addition of skins and fur in winter; woolen cloth is used sparingly, and is not manufactured by the Chinese. Leather is used in some parts of

CHINESE TAILOR.

the empire for the soles of shoes, but felt is more common. The shoes worn by laborers appear very clumsy to a foreigner, and are stiff and heavy. The women wear shoes made of silk with felt soles, and of a ridiculously small size.

The chief articles of dress worn by the Chinese men are inner and outer tunics of various lengths, made of cotton or silk, reaching below the loins, frequently extending to the feet. The lapel folds over the breast and is fastened on the left side. The neck is left uncovered. The sleeves, much wider and longer than the arms, have no cuffs or facings, and are used for pockets. It is astonishing how many articles a Chinaman can stow away in the sleeves of his dress. In robes of ceremony the ends of the sleeves are cut to resemble a horse's hoof. The lower part of the body is covered by a pair of loose trousers made of silk or satin, with cloth stockings reaching to the knees. In winter leggings are added to keep the lower limbs comfortable. The thick felt soles of shoes are intended to keep the feet dry and warm in the absence of fire; not for ornament, certainly. One writer has said, speaking of their shoes, that "the Chinese carry the floors of their houses on the soles of their feet."

The ancient Chinese suffered their hair to grow long, and bound it in a neat coil on top of the head. The present style of shaving the head and wearing the cue was imposed upon them by their conquerors, the Manchoo Tartars. The head is shaved to the crown, and the hair carefully braided in a single plait behind. The Chinese hat indicates the literary grade or official rank of the wearer. The head is usually covered in winter by a silk skullcap, or felt hat of peculiar shape. Most men go bareheaded in summer, especially in the southern provinces. Outdoor laborers wear in summer an umbrella-shaped hat, made of bamboo, and very large. It is a good protection from the fierce heat of the sun. Head coverings, however, vary in different parts of the empire according to climate, taste, or convenience.

The dress of the women in China, like that of the men, does not change with the phases of the moon, but remains substantially the same through many generations. The fashion is sure to last as long as the gown. The dresses of the common people, men and women, resemble each other so much that a stranger is at a loss to distinguish one from the other. For this reason I shall not dwell upon the subject of female dress. Besides, I have neither the information nor the genius to discuss successfully so delicate and difficult a subject. There *are* differences, of course, between the dresses of the men and the women, which, on better acquaintance, become evident enough. The women seldom wear white, blue being their favorite color. The headdress of married females is very becoming. No caps, bonnets, hoods, or veils are worn abroad; a light umbrella is used to protect them from the sun. Bangles, bracelets, and earrings are worn by all classes, more as amulets to ward off evil influences than as ornaments.

The cramping of the feet of female children is one of the strangest customs in China. There is a difference of opinion among writers on the subject as to the origin of this absurd custom. Some say that it arose from a desire to flatter a popular empress of China who had club feet. Others say that it gradually came into use from the great desire among the women to have small feet. Again it is said that it was imposed upon them by their husbands to keep them from gadding about. We doubt this. Women are not so easily " imposed

CHINESE SHOEMAKER.

upon" by their husbands, even in China. When the Manchoo Tartars took possession of China, before they had really subdued all the provinces, they ordered the men in China to have their heads shaved and wear the cue, as a sign of allegiance to the new dynasty, on penalty of death; and that the women change the manner of fastening their outer tunics. The men, it is said, obeyed the order promptly; but the women obstinately refused, and though many of them were put to death, they would not yield, and continued to fasten their dresses as their grandmothers did, and as every Chinese woman does to-day. Whatever be the facts as to the history of cramping the feet, I take it the women adopted the practice voluntarily. It is certainly a very extraordinary custom, and one for which it is impossible to see any good reason. It must be very painful; it disfigures the person, renders walking difficult, and has no compensating benefits; yet the Chinese women adhere obstinately to the practice. I have seen grown women, who were mothers, wearing shoes not more than three inches long. They could not walk with any ease or grace. Many cannot even hobble along without assistance, yet they not only endure the pain and inconvenience themselves, but inflict the horrid custom upon their daughters while children.

The Chinese women use cosmetics to beautify their faces, but really and practically to the serious injury of the skin. When in full dress, the face is entirely covered with white paint, except the cheeks and lips, which are touched with rouge. This gives the countenance an unnatural appearance, as if it had been whitewashed. The belle is described as having " cheeks like almond flowers, lips like the peach bloom, a waist as the willow leaf, eyes bright as dancing ripples in the sun, and footsteps like the lotus flower." An American writer thus describes a well-dressed Chinese gentleman: "He wears by his side a variety of accouterments, which strike a stranger as being of a warlike character, but on closer inspection prove to be very peaceful appendages. A worked silk sheath incloses a fan; a small leather bag, not unlike a cartouch box, suspended to the belt, supplies flint and steel for lighting his pipe; and the tobacco is carried in an embroidered purse or pouch." Although thus arrayed, and easily mistaken for a walking armory, he is one of the most harmless creatures of his kind in the land. He is simply a well-dressed Chinaman.

STREET RESTAURANT.

## CHAPTER XVI.

### Diet of the Chinese.

THE Chinese are not cannibals, nor are they wild savages eating their food raw. They know how to cook and how to eat. Their fondness for puppies, cats, rats, snakes, etc., has been greatly exaggerated. In some provinces in the south, and it may be in other parts of the empire, such creatures are used for food, but in eastern China, about Shanghai, I never saw or heard of such a thing. Men are seen on the streets of Shanghai with rats in baskets, and, like the common hucksters, have a peculiar cry; but they are rat-catchers, and not rat-sellers. They will clear your house of rats in a short time for a few cents, but they do not eat rats, nor sell them to other people to be eaten. A stranger, seeing one of these " rat-catchers " passing along the street, and hearing his cry, and being ignorant of his language, naturally supposes he wishes to sell his rats; and for what purpose, if not for food? Dr. Williams says of Canton: "A few kittens and puppies are sold alive in baskets, mewing and yelping as if in anticipation of their fate, or from pain caused by pinching and handling them," etc. It is true, therefore, that some Chinese do eat rats, kittens, and puppies, but such food is by no means common.

The common diet of the Chinese is sufficient in variety, in wholesomeness, and in quantity to furnish a very comfortable *menu*. The method of preparing their food does not always please a foreign palate; neither does our method please the Chinese taste. Our cheese, for instance, they cannot tolerate for a moment; and so also of our butter, and other dishes. The free use of vegetable oil in the preparation of most Chinese dishes is offensive to foreigners. Every nation has its own method of cooking food, building houses, making clothes, and in these matters the Chinese have equal rights with the rest of mankind.

The proportion of animal food used by the Chinese is perhaps less than in most countries covering the same degrees of latitude. Of course the quality as well as the quantity consumed by a family depends upon the means of supply. The rich may have anything the market can furnish; the poor must be content with what their limited finances can afford. A Chinese table seems to a foreigner poorly supplied, with no bread, butter, or milk. Rice is always present. Tea is used in great quantities by all classes, and is always taken hot with no sugar or cream, and a weak decoction is preferred.

The Chinese have a long list of culinary vegetables. Many sorts of peas and beans are cultivated. They have a peculiar dish, very popular with the people, called "bean curd." In the latitude favorable to their growth cabbage, kale, cauliflower, cress, lettuce, spinach, celery, dandelion, sweet basil, purslane, clover, onions, pumpkins, squashes, turnips, eggplant, melons of all kinds, sweet potatoes, cucumbers, water-chestnuts, ginger, mustard, radishes, garlic, leeks, chives, etc., are raised by farmers and gardeners in great quantities. Irish potatoes and Indian maize have been introduced into China within the last half century.

Most of the fruits common in the tropics and in the temperate zones are found in China. The shaddock, plantain, and persimmon are common. The persimmon is a luscious fruit, several times as large as in this country. The pomegranate, mango, custard apple, pineapple, breadfruit, fig, guava, olive, grape, etc., are abundant in their several localities. Chestnuts, walnuts, filberts, and almonds are the most common nuts. The blackberry, strawberry, raspberry, arbutus, and cranberry are found in several of the provinces. The Chinese have long known how to preserve fruits and to pickle vegetables. The common beverages of the Chinese are tea and whisky, and both are taken warm; cold water is seldom drank, because supposed to be unwholesome. Beer, cider, porter, wine, and brandy are unknown, except as introduced by foreigners. Coffee and chocolate are never used.

Beef is not a common meat, chiefly because the government protects the ox for the use of the farmer, and also because of the Buddhist prejudice against killing such a noble animal. Mutton is rare and expensive. The meat of the water buffalo and of the goat are seldom eaten. More pork is eaten than any other kind of meat. Few families are so poor as not to have a pig. Horse flesh and venison are now and then seen in the markets. Pork, fowls, and fish are staple articles of diet. Ducks, chickens, and geese are abundant. The turkey is not found in China. Pheasants, grouse, and quail are plentiful in some parts of the country. Frogs are eaten by all classes. A writer thus describes a curious way of catching frogs: "A young and tender jumper is caught and tied to a fish line and bobbed up and down in the rice field where the old croakers are wont to harbor. As soon as one sees the young frog he makes a plunge at him and swallows him whole, whereupon he is immediately landed in the fisherman's basket, and so loses his lunch and his life together, for the young frog is rescued from his maw and used again as bait."

The eggs of chickens and ducks are hatched artificially in every part of the empire. The process of hatching is simple, only requiring constant attention. Sheds are erected for the purpose, in which is a number of baskets well plastered with mud, each one so placed over a fire that the heat shall be conveyed equally to the eggs through tiles placed in the bottom of the basket, and retained by a close cover. The heat is raised to about one hundred Fahrenheit and continued for four or five days. The eggs are then taken out and each one carefully examined in a strong light. Those "addled" are left out, and the sound ones replaced in the basket, and kept for ten days longer, when they are placed on shelves in the center of the shed and covered with cotton and felt for fourteen days longer. At the end of twenty-eight days the little ducks and chickens break the shell and come forth. They are immediately sold to persons whose business it is to feed and care for them until ready for the market. Pigeons are raised to some extent, their eggs being used for soups. The wild duck, teal, wild goose, plover, snipe, partridge, are all eaten by the Chinese. If the Chinese eat many sorts of birds and beasts that live on the land, the variety of fish and other productions of the water which they consume is still greater. Nothing comes amiss. The right to fish in running water is open to all, and besides this the lakes and seas are free. Artificial ponds, pools, tanks, etc., are used for rearing fish by private individuals and by companies. Crabs, cuttle fish, sharks, turtles, prawns, crawfish, rays, and shrimps are all used for food by rich and poor.

I have thus dwelt upon the diet of the Chinese because the most common question asked me after my return from China was, "What do the Chinese eat?" or, "How do the millions of Chinese manage to obtain food enough for all?" Of course it is a serious question among the masses in all countries, and especially where the population is so dense as in China. To feed four hundred millions of people so that everyone shall have a little, requires an amount of food greatly beyond our powers of computation. An American missionary some years ago made an estimate of the amount of rice necessary to furnish every man, woman, and child in China one meal, and found that all the rice raised in the United States would barely be sufficient, allowing one pint of cooked rice to each person!

The culinary art has not been cultivated in China with any great success. The principal dishes are stews of various kinds, in which garlic and grease are more abundant than pepper and salt. Meats are seldom baked or roasted, owing partly, no doubt, to the greater amount of fuel required to bake than to fry. Fuel is very expensive in many parts of the empire, hence the poor can better afford to buy the little meat they use, already cooked, than to cook it themselves. The articles of kitchen furniture in a dwelling are few and simple. An iron boiler shaped like a wash basin, for stewing or frying, a portable earthen furnace, and two or three different-shaped earthenware pots for boiling water or vegetables, constitute the whole culinary establishment of thousands of households. Meats or vegetables are hashed or cut into small blocks before being brought to the table. They do not use knives and forks in eating, as we do, but manage to convey all kinds of food to their mouths by the "chopsticks"—two small sticks, each abut the size and shape of an ordinary lead pencil.

The manner of eating their food differs as much among the Chinese as among other people. With the humble poor the question is how to provide food, and there is very little form or ceremony in preparing or eating it. Rice is the "staff of life." The poor seldom taste meat; sometimes a small piece of fish is placed in the bowl of rice; sometimes vegetables are added, to give flavor to the dish; a little garlic or piece of onion very greatly increases the relish. As a rule the Chinese do not eat early in the day; usually about eleven o'clock, and again at night. They are a social and sensual people, and the pleasures of the table form a principal part of their enjoyment where they have the means to gratify the appetite to the full. They are not convivial—that is, intoxicants are not used to excess; they may be gluttons, but they are not drunkards. Private meals and public feasts among the wealthy are both dull and tedious. The intellect is subordinate to the appetite. There is no "feast of reason" nor "flow of soul" at a Chinese dinner. There may be "small talk" and commonplace twaddle enough, but the social vivacity, wit, and humor that characterize fashionable dinings with us are unknown among the higher classes in China. There are no ladies present, and therefore the principal charm of a social meeting with us is conspicuously absent at a Chinese feast. The men are simply "animals feeding," though with much parade of etiquette and elaborate formality.

The beggars in China, like mendicants in all

countries, "live from hand to mouth," and are often driven by extreme hunger to eat the vilest refuse: cats, dogs, rats, snakes, lizzards, slugs, decayed meats and vegetables, etc. Extremes of wealth and poverty are often seen in painful contrast in China.

CHINESE CART.

## CHAPTER XVII.

### Agriculture in China.

AGRICULTURE occupies the first place with the Chinese among the industrial arts, and it is annually honored by the government when the emperor becomes, for the hour, a practical farmer, and holds the plow.* This ceremony is observed with much imperial pomp, in order to impress not only the farm laborer with the dignity and importance of his vocation, but to remind the whole nation of the place which agriculture holds as the primary source of supply for human wants, and that from which national wealth and comfort are derived. The simplest form of manual labor is thus selected as representative of all labor, and the highest honor bestowed upon it. One Chinese writer has classified the different occupations thus: "1. The *scholar:* because mind is superior to matter, and it is the intellect that distinguishes man above the lower order of beings, and enables him to provide food and raiment and shelter for himself and for other creatures. 2. The *farmer:* because the mind cannot act without the body, and

---

*Once a year the emperor and his ministers "plow the sacred field" with a highly ornamented plow. The emperor turns three furrows, the princes five, and the imperial ministers nine. The ground belongs to the temples of heaven and earth, and the crop of wheat raised on the field is used in idolatrous services.

the body cannot exist without food, so that farming is essential to the existence of man, especially in civilized society. 3. The *mechanic:* because, next to food, shelter is a necessity, and the man who builds a house comes next in honor to the man who furnishes food. 4. The *tradesman:* because, as society increases, and its wants are multiplied, men to carry on exchange and barter become a necessity, and so the merchant comes into existence. His occupation—shaving both sides, the producer and the consumer—tempts him to act dishonestly, hence his low grade. 5. The *soldier* stands last and lowest in the list, because his business is to destroy and not to build up society. He consumes what others produce, but produces nothing himself that can benefit mankind. He is, perhaps, a necessary evil."

The above sketch is reproduced from memory, and may not be in every respect exactly accurate. I do not recall the author. I understand, however, this to be the theory of the Chinese government in regard to the relative importance and dignity of the several professions, and it is creditable to the good sense of the nation. Notwithstanding the honor thus conferred upon the farmer theoretically, farming in China is not more pleasant or profitable than in other countries. Indeed, there are no large farmers in China. The Chinese are gardeners, and not farmers. The density of the population and the methods of cultivation make small farms or gardens a necessity.

The land in China is held as a freehold so long as the government receives the taxes, or "rent," as the tax is called. This amounts to about one-tenth of the produce raised on the land. The tax on land in the city is estimated in the same way, and is relatively very small. The government manages, however, in other ways to make the rich men of the city bear their proportion of the national expenses. The local authorities "squeeze" (by a system of "borrowing") the wealthy men of the community. If the mandarins ask the loan of a few hundred dollars, or it may be a few thousand, the merchant or tradesman from whom the "loan" is asked knows better than to refuse to comply. His refusal might render it necessary to employ other means that would greatly embarrass him, for there are more ways than one of squeezing a rich man in China. In this manner the burden of taxation is distributed among all classes, and thus the excessive pressure on the landholder is mitigated.

The legal sources of revenue, besides the land tax, are custom and transit duties, pawnbroker's taxes, "taxes on frontier and transportation," salt department (salt is a government monopoly), custom duties on foreign trade, etc. The parental estate and the houses upon it descend to the oldest son, but his brothers can remain upon it with their families, and devise their portion in perpetuity to their children. So that a Chinese farmer feels secure in his home so long as he can pay the tax upon it. The country people, as a rule, are poor and very ignorant. When a city man would express his contempt for anyone whom he wishes to degrade, he calls him " a countryman " —or a farmer.

The implements used in agriculture by the Chinese are few and exceedingly rude; the hoe, the mattock, spade, and shovel, with a miserable substitute for a plow, constitute the outfit of the average farmer. He makes up for the disadvantages of poor instruments by hard work. The buffalo, ox, horse, and mule are used in farming to some extent, but not as much as with us. You will sometimes see two of these animals yoked together in a ludicrous manner, and the driver arrayed in a fantastic suit woven of straw, and resembling somewhat a walking haystack. The clumsy plow barely scratches the surface of the ground, but the soil is fertile, and the climate friendly, so that in the end the industrious farmer gathers in a good harvest as the reward of his toil.

Rice is the principal article of food in China, and its production is therefore general wherever the conditions are at all favorable to its growth. The manner of raising it need not here be described, because there is nothing peculiar about it. Wheat, barley, and millet are grown in large quantities. The demand for food in China is so great that the farmer gives little attention comparatively to any other product than grain and vegetables, except, perhaps, cotton, hemp, indigo, tea, and some others, used in manufactures and commerce. The celebrated "nankeen cotton" is raised in the great valley of the Yang-tse. I have seen it and a very fair article of white cotton growing side by side near Shanghai.

I shall omit any description of the manner in which the ordinary farm products are cultivated, because there is nothing strikingly peculiar about it. Of all the branches of Chinese industry, the growth and preparation of tea has been the most celebrated, and is one of the most important to China and to Western nations.

### GROWTH AND PREPARATION OF THE TEA PLANT.

The knowledge of the tea plant cannot be traced farther back than A.D. 350. Its general use among the Chinese dates back to A.D. 800. It is related to the Camellia, and bears the same name among the Chinese. It usually grows from three to six feet high, and presents a dense foliage, the result of frequent pruning. In Assam, where it grows wild, it often reaches the height of thirty feet. The leaf is of a dark green color, of an oblong oval shape, and the flowers are white, single, and without odor. The seeds are like hazel nuts in size and color, three of them being inclosed in a hard husk, and so oily as to soon become rancid. The tea plant resembles in appearance the privet of our hedges.

The soil most favorable to the growth of the tea plant is a rich, sandy earth, with a large proportion of vegetable mold in it. The hillside is preferred to the lower ground, if near water; and usually the patches above rice fields furnish the best flavored leaves. It is from orchards thus situated that the most celebrated brands of tea are obtained. The greater part of the tea exported is grown in the provinces of Fo-keen, Che-kiang, and Kiang-su. It is, however, produced in all the eighteen provinces except in the extreme north. It is usually raised by individual farmers, who cultivate a few dozen—or, it may be, a few score—of shrubs upon their own lands, and either cure the leaves themselves or sell them to their neighbors, who prepare them for the market. There are a few large plantations under the care of rich landlords, but not many. The small farmer raises tea as he does cotton, silk, or rice, and when the season ends sells to the tea broker, who carries it to the best market he can find.

A single plant or tree of large size will produce annually from sixteen to twenty-four ounces of leaves. Three crops are gathered during the season. The first picking takes place about the middle of April, or whenever the tender buds begin to open, and while the leaves are still covered with a whitish down. These early pickings produce the best tea. The second gathering is about the first of May, when the shrubs are covered with full-grown leaves. The Chinese say that the weather affects very materially the quality of the leaves, and that when the proper time comes the picking should be done as rapidly as possible. The leaves are put into a basket and taken to the curing houses. The third and last picking of leaves takes place in July. There is "a gleaning" or picking in August, called "autumn dew," which produces an inferior quality of tea. The quality of the different kinds of tea depends upon the nature of the soil, climate, age of the leaf, and the manner of curing.

TEA-CURING HOUSE.

After the leaves are gathered and housed, they are carefully assorted, the yellow and old ones picked out. The remainder of the "picking" is spread on bamboo trays, and placed where the wind can blow upon them until they begin to soften; then, while lying upon the tray, they are gently rolled and rubbed for some time, when red spots appear upon them. They are then tested by pouring hot water upon them to see if the edge of the leaf turns yellow. The leaves must be rolled many times, and then " fired." The pan in which the leaves are to be put is heated to a proper temperature, and the workman takes a handful of leaves and sprinkles them upon it and waits until each leaf " pops," when he instantly brushes them off before they are charred. Such is the account which the Chinese give of the manner in which the tea is prepared in the Bohea hills. The testing and rolling are omitted in preparing the common sorts of tea. The fresh leaves are thrown into the heated pans and kept in motion until the oil is forced out and they burst open. After four or five minutes they are taken out and rolled. This operation is performed on tables made of split bamboos. After the leaves are thus rolled they are shaken out loosely and placed on trays to complete the necessary drying.* The common sorts of black tea are left in the sun and air after the first process of firing and rolling, a much longer time—even for days, especially if the tea is intended for the foreign market.

As soon as the process of curing is finished, the finer quality is inclosed in canisters or small paper bags, and packed in boxes lined with lead. The tea is then ready for the broker, who purchases it directly from the producer, and carries it to some seaport where it is prepared for shipment to for-

---

*Dr. Williams; Chinese Repository.

eign countries, or sold to Chinese merchants for home consumption.

The question is often asked whether the different kinds of tea come from the same shrub, or whether there are varieties of the same plant—a black tea plant, and a green tea plant, etc. There is but one plant, from which all the kinds of tea known to the trade are made. The differences which characterize each kind are the result of the manner in which the leaf is manipulated. Green tea is cured more rapidly than black tea, and is not thrown into baskets after it is fired. Green tea can be changed into black tea, but black tea cannot be changed into green tea. More of the essential oil remains in the green tea than in the black, and this is the cause, perhaps, of the difference in the flavor of the two kinds.

There may be some difference in the peculiar quality of the plant, caused by a difference of soil and climate, for it is raised over a large extent of country, covering several degrees of latitude; but the difference cannot be detected in the leaf when green or dried. Tea is a universal beverage in China and Japan, and is used extensively in Mongolia, Siam, and other neighboring countries. It is regarded as very wholesome by the Chinese, and is used as a substitute for cold water as a drink. Tea shops are seen everywhere in cities, towns, and villages, and even in the hamlets throughout the rural districts. Everybody drinks tea everywhere and at all times.

CHINESE LOOM.

REELING SILK.

## CHAPTER XVIII.

### MANUFACTURES IN CHINA.

#### *PORCELAIN.*

THE Chinese are an ingenious people, and in no department of industry have they displayed their originality more than in their arts and manufactures. In early discoveries and inventions they have no rivals. Long before the mariner's compass was known in the West they were using the magnetic needle in their sedan chairs and carriages. So also of the composition of gunpowder and the art of printing. However much we have surpassed them in the practical use and improvement of these inventions, we must admit the priority of the Chinese claim to be the original inventors. It is reasonable to suppose that the knowledge of these contrivances traveled slowly by tradition from China into Europe, and that the world is indebted to these ingenious Asiatics for the three great discoveries, or inventions. Porcelain may be classed with printing, the compass, and gunpowder, as an original Chinese invention.

The word porcelain, from the Portuguese *porcellana*, means seashell, and was the name given by the Portuguese to the semi-transparent cups which they saw on their arrival in China. It is therefore another name for China ware. The following account of the manufacture of porcelain is taken from Sir John Davis's History of China. I have seen all varieties of Chinese and Japanese ware, but I never saw a porcelain factory, and cannot therefore describe the process of manufacture from my own personal knowledge:

"Silica and alumina, or flint and clay, are the principal constituents in all China ware. The Chinese say that they procure the material for the manufacture of porcelain from a high mountain in the neighborhood of Poyang lake. Foreigners have examined this material and find it to be felspar and clay, or the same as the porcelain earth of Europe. The silica is reduced by pounding in mortars to a very fine powder. This is made into paste and sold to the manufacturers of porcelain. Another substance used in making the ware is soapstone; and still another is alabaster, or gypsum, which is used in painting the articles manufactured.

"The vitreous glaze used by the Chinese to finish off their porcelain is obtained by mixing the powdered silica or flint with the ashes of fern. They call this 'varnish.' In painting the ware one set of people design the outline and others fill in the colors. The Chinese say the object of this arrangement is to 'concentrate the workman's hand, and not divide his mind.' It is said that previous to baking the same specimen of ware passes through twenty hands, and that before being sold it has gone through more than double that number.

The colors used on the finest quality of porcelain have long been admired by foreigners, and efforts have frequently been made to ascertain the material used and the manner of mixing the colors. Enough has been learned, however, to enable the European manufacturers to equal, if not surpass, the Chinese artists in ornamenting their work, whether they have discovered the Chinese secret or not. The Japanese have long understood the art of manufacturing porcelain, and have excelled the Chinese in design and execution."

Besides table furniture, jars of various sizes and shapes have been manufactured by the Chinese both for use and ornament. Porcelain idols are common in the homes and temples; the God of Porcelain himself is usually made of this material. The tradition concerning this god is that a certain workman was ordered by the emperor to produce some vases of peculiar fineness. After several unsuccessful efforts to secure the desired quality, the workman became desperate, and in his frenzy leaped into the furnace and was instantly consumed. The vases that came out of the furnace after the immolation of the workman pleased the emperor so much that he deified him. A cheap stoneware is made by the Chinese for common use. Large jars for holding grain, water, etc., are to be seen in all parts of China about the homes of the rich and poor. They are very substantial, and often sufficiently large to hold fifty gallons of water or grain.

### LACQUER WARE.

The beautiful lacquered ware, which foreigners admire so much, though not made of porcelain, may be classed with the same grade of manufactures, because, like the porcelain, it combines the two qualities of the useful and ornamental. The Japanese surpass all the rest of the world in the production of this peculiar ware. They learned the art from the Chinese, but have far excelled their teachers. Cabinets, secretaries, writing desks, jewelry boxes, and hundreds of other designs, are manufactured by the Chinese for the foreign markets of the West. Whatever the design may be, the manner of making the article is the same. The body of the ware is wood partially smoothed, or it may be pasteboard, upon which two or three coats of a composition of lime, paper, and gum are first laid and thoroughly dried and rubbed. The surface of the wood is also hardened by rubbing coarse clay upon it, and afterwards scraping it off. Two coatings of lampblack and wood oil, or of lampblack and varnish, are now laid on, one after the other, with great care in close and darkened rooms, allowing it to dry well between the several coats. The articles are then laid by to be painted and gilded according to the fancy of the artist, after which a last coating is given them. A very beautiful quality of lacquered ware is made by inlaying with mother-of-pearl taken from salt and fresh water shells. Another kind, much admired by the Chinese, is made by covering the wood with a coating of red varnish three or four lines in thickness, and then carving figures upon it in relief. This kind of ware is expensive.

### MANUFACTURE OF SILK.

The Chinese were the first people to manufacture silk, as they were the inventors of porcelain and lacquered ware, and in neither have foreigners yet excelled them. The French China ware is very beautiful, but it is said to be inferior in some important respects to that manufactured in China.

The cultivation of the mulberry tree and the manufacture of silk can be traced back to seven hundred and eighty years before our era. Indeed, the Chinese historians refer the invention of weaving silk to the Empress Siling, the wife of the Emperor Wangte, B.C. 2602. However this may be, nobody doubts that the Chinese were the original inventors, and the intelligent world has agreed to give them the credit of it. How the silkworm was discovered, and what suggested the use of the cocoon; how the mulberry leaf was found to be the natural food for the worm, etc., we are not informed. The Chinese have always been careful and patient observers of nature, with a practical turn of mind which sought to improve every fact for some useful purpose. It is said by one of their classical writers that "in ancient times emperors plowed the lands and empresses cultivated the mulberry. Though the most honorable, they did not disdain to toil and labor, as examples to

CHINESE ARTIST.

EMBROIDERING.

the whole empire, in order to induce all the people to seek these essential supports."

The finest silk in the world is said to be produced in the province of Hoo-peh in China. Great care is taken in rearing the silkworms, and in cultivating the mulberry leaves upon which they feed. While the worms are growing, and also while they are spinning, they are kept in absolute quiet—all noise is forbidden in their neighborhood. They are often changed from one hurdle to another, in order to keep them clean and to give them pure air. The worms must be fed at the right time, and in sufficient quantity. The mulberry leaf must be of the proper kind, age, and condition. Three days are required for them to spin, and in six days the larvæ must be stifled and the silk reeled from the cocoons. This, however, is usually done by other workmen than those who rear the worms. The cocoons are placed in a jar and buried in the ground, being interlarded with a layer of leaves and salt, which kills the pupæ and keeps the silk supple, strong, and lustrous. Preserved in this manner, the cocoons can be transported to any distance. The cocoons are sometimes spread on trays and exposed to the steam of boiling water. After exposure to steam, the silk can be reeled off without difficulty.

Che-kiang province produces the finest silk, next to the province of Hoo-peh, and this is attributed, in part at least, to the superior quality of the mulberry leaf on which the worms feed. The silk is rich and the country well watered; the climate seems also well adapted to produce a tender and delicate leaf, and the people have for ages given themselves almost wholly to the growing of silk, so that this province is celebrated in the silk markets of the world for the superior quality of its raw silk. The proportion of food favorable to the growth and productiveness of the worms has been accurately ascertained by experience, and the leaves are carefully weighed as they are fed to the worms.

Large quantities of raw silk are sent out of the country, especially to France, but the principal part is woven into fabrics in China. The Chinese loom is a peculiar machine, and exceedingly simple in structure, yet capable of producing marvelous results in the hands of skilled native workmen. It requires two men to work it, one of whom sits on the top of the frame and manages the treadles, and the other sits below and superintends the changes necessary to form the desired pattern. They will imitate almost any design, excelling especially in crapes, flowered satins, and damasks. Many of the delicate silk tissues known in Europe are not made in China, most of their fabrics being heavy gauze.

Chinese embroidery is well known, and celebrated for its delicacy and beauty throughout the civilized world. It is used a great deal in China to adorn the dresses of the officers, from the emperor down to the lowest grade; also for ladies' dresses, purses, shoes, caps, fans, and other articles. All the work is done by hand, unaided by any sort of machinery except a light frame on which the material is stretched. There are many styles of work, all more or less beautiful. I have seen women at work on the most elegant fabrics, doing the finest style of embroidery, in miserable hovels, surrounded by all the inconveniences and discomforts of abject poverty. It is a mystery how they keep from soiling the delicate silks and satins on which they work. Much of the most elegant embroidery is made by poor women.

BRIDE AND BRIDEGROOM.

# CHAPTER XIX.

## SOCIAL AND DOMESTIC LIFE IN CHINA.

### BETROTHAL AND MARRIAGE.

THERE can be no pure social or domestic life where woman is degraded; where she is bought and sold as a chattel, and where she is treated in her own home as a menial. Where woman is degraded man is degraded. The separation of the sexes debases man as well as woman. The men become coarse, selfish, and brutal; the women cultivate gossip, indolence, and the vices peculiar to an unnatural and restrained mode of life. In China the separation of the sexes has led the men to spend their idle time in gambling and opium smoking. Other kindred vices have followed, until the whole fabric of social life has sunk to the lowest depths of moral degradation. That the women should be pure and virtuous, where the men are so demoralized, is hardly to be expected.

In giving some account of the social and domestic life of the Chinese, it will be well to begin with marriage, as this is the foundation of all organized and well-regulated society. The Chinese have always observed and honored the marriage relation, and the laws of the empire have carefully guarded the sanctity and duties of the institution. Although a modified form of polygamy is permitted in certain cases, a man can have but one *legal* wife in China. He may purchase concubines, but they sustain the relation of servants in the family, and not that of wives.

Betrothal in China takes the place of courtship in our country. The young people may never see each other until after marriage; indeed, they cannot unless by accident, or in a clandestine way. The whole matter is a pure business transaction, conducted by the parents of the parties and the go-between. There may be love between the husband and wife after they have become acquainted, but there is no opportunity for such a thing before marriage.

Six formal ceremonies are to be observed in all regular betrothals. (1) The father and elder brother of the boy or young man who would seek a bride send a "go-between" (the person who conducts the negotiations between the parties) to the father and brother of the girl selected, to inquire her name and the moment of her birth, in order that the horoscopes of the two may be examined and compared by the astrologer, to see if their union as husband and wife would be fortunate. (2) If the astrologer pronounces the conditions to be favorable, the go-between is sent back to make an offer of marriage to the father and brother of the girl. (3) If he is accepted, the second party is requested to put their answer in writing. (4) Presents are then sent to the girl's parents according to the social rank and ability of the two families. (5) The go-between now requests the parties to select a lucky day for the wedding. (6) When the day selected for the marriage arrives the bridegroom sends a party of his friends with a red sedan chair and a band of musicians to bring the bride to his own house.

In some parts of the country mere infants are sometimes betrothed, and the transaction is registered, containing the names of the children, the particulars of their birth, etc.; and these registers are exchanged by the parents of the children in testimony of the contract. After this has been done, unless one of the parties becomes a leper, or is disabled, it is impossible to retract the engagement. When the persons betrothed are older, the boy sometimes accompanies the go-between and the party carrying the presents to the house of the future mother-in-law, and receives from her some trifling articles, as melon seeds, fruits, etc., which he distributes to those present. Among the presents sent to the girl are fruits, money, vermicelli, and a ham, of which she gives a morsel to each person, and sends the foot back. The party bringing these presents is received with a salute of firecrackers. What it all means we are not informed, except that custom demands that these ceremonies be observed as preliminary to marriage.

After the time of engagement the girl is required to maintain the strictest seclusion. When friends call she must retire to the inner apartments, and on all occasions conduct herself with rigid decorum according to the ancient rites. When she goes out it must be in a close sedan chair, and her intercourse with her brothers and the domestics of the household must be governed by extreme reserve. She is deprived of those delightful friendships and associations with her own sex and age which render young womanhood in the West such a happy season. The Chinese young girl, thus secluded and fenced in by custom, has no opportunity to form acquaintances outside of her own family before marriage, and after marriage she is doomed to strict privacy. Such, at least, is the theory of Chinese domestic life so far as the females of the household are concerned.

The rites and ceremonies connected with a legal marriage in China are substantially the same in all the provinces, modified, however, more or less by local customs. The ceremonies here described are those observed in a southern province, and may differ in a few particulars from what is observed at weddings in some other provinces, but in no *essential* point.

The marriage cannot take place until all the presents due from the bridegroom have been received. These are sometimes costly, amounting to hundreds of dollars, but usually, among the well-to-do classes, the sum does not exceed twenty-five to forty dollars.

When the lucky day arrives, all the preliminaries having been satisfactorily arranged, the invited guests assemble in the house of the bridegroom, where musicians, sedans, and porters are in readiness. The courier, who acts as guide to the chair-bearers, takes the lead of the procession, and in order to prevent evil spirits from doing mischief to the party he carries a baked pig, or large piece of pork; and while the spirits are supposed to be devouring the meat, the company passes on unharmed. In the meantime the bride has been properly arrayed, and is ready for the chair-bearers who are to bear her to the bridegroom's house. An elaborate and ornamental headdress, made of rich materials, resembling in general appearance a crown, forms a part of the trousseau. A large red mantle covers her person. Thus attired, she enters the "flowery chair," and is borne away to her future home, there to meet for the first time her husband. She "weeps and wails" all the way, for it would be unbecoming to show any signs of pleasure on leaving her father and mother and the home of her childhood. The weeping is conventional, but often sincere, no doubt; for she is going she knows not where, and to meet new trials, and perhaps new sorrows. She is to become the slave of her husband; and what may be worse, she is to become the drudge of a bad-tempered mother-in-law. But she has no choice in the matter—all has been arranged for her by others, and her duty is simply to do as she is bid. It always has been so with her, and it will be to the end of life. She has no rights that anybody is bound to respect; she is only a woman, a creature without a soul and without a future. No wonder she weeps!

The procession leaves the bride's home, carrying all the worldly goods which the means of the family will allow. These things are usually packed in red boxes. The courier hastens on to announce the approach of the procession, whereupon the music strikes up, and the inevitable firecrackers are let off until she enters the gate. The go-between brings forward a young child to meet her, while she goes in search of the bridegroom who is supposed to have concealed himself. When he meets the bride, they—both bridegroom and bride—approach the ancestral tablets of his ancestors and worship, bowing three times in a most reverent and solemn manner. They then seat themselves at a table on which are two cups of wine. The go-between serves them, and they both taste the wine. This is the *legal* point in the marriage ceremony—" pledging the wine cup." It is never omitted. After this part of the ceremony has been performed by the go-between, any other local ceremonies may be introduced. Then the bride is conducted to the bridal chamber, and her veil is removed. The bridegroom enters and looks upon her for a moment and retires. The female guests and friends now enter, and are at liberty to criticise the person of the bride, which they usually do with entire freedom. As before stated, customs vary in different provinces. In some places the ceremonies are much more elaborate than in others, and many local superstitions are observed in one province wholly unknown in other provinces. The rich make it an occasion for displaying their wealth. The poor are unable to do more than imitate the rich as far as their limited means will permit. Among the poor, in order to avoid the expenses of a wedding, a girl is sometimes purchased for a small sum, and brought up in the family as a daughter until she reaches a marriageable age, when she becomes a wife with simple and inexpensive ceremonies. In this, as in other matters, the rich do as they please, while the poor do the best they can. Happiness does not depend upon wealth or honors anywhere. The Chinese are under the same natural and moral laws, and subject to the same providential government, with ourselves, and we find therefore similar experiences in all conditions of life here and in China: the rich are often miserable, and the poor comparatively happy. Of course the conditions of social life are in Christian countries vastly more favorable to the happiness of all classes than in heathen lands. I speak only relatively when I compare Chinese social and domestic life with our own. The comparison amounts to a painful contrast. In China woman is degraded and all associated with her is demoralized. There is not among the unconverted millions of China a single *home*, in the sense in which we use that sweet word. There are millions of households, but not homes, for the wife and mother and her daughters are regarded as inferiors, as servants, whose sole duty it is to provide for the comfort of the male members of the family, and not as equals or companions. There are, no doubt, exceptions to this unhappy state of domestic life. The wife may not feel that any injustice is done her, and that she ought therefore to be content with her lot. All husbands are not tyrannical and cruel, and some mothers-in-law may be gentle and patient, but the conditions generally are not favorable to domestic felicity.

Concubines are not married with the ceremonies just described, but are simply purchased and brought into the family as inferiors or domestics. If they have children the legal wife is accounted the *mother*, and the children address her as such, and they have equal rights with the children born of the wife. The Chinese are aware of the evils of a divided household, and the law places the authority to control all the members of the family in the hands of the wife. This does not, however, prevent domestic jealousies, bickerings, and strifes, especially if the concubines live under the same roof with the wife. Polygamy is esteemed one of the luxuries of the rich, and is seldom found among the poor.

If a betrothed girl loses her intended husband by death, public opinion honors her if she refuse a second engagement. So strong is this feeling that girls have been known to commit suicide rather than contract a second marriage. Sometimes, after a girl has been betrothed, the circumstances of her own family and those of her intended husband are so changed that they are no longer in the same social grade; or it may be he has become dissipated and worthless, and totally unworthy of the girl—still the contract must be fulfilled; there is no escape for the poor girl except in death, and too often the wretched bride commits suicide to escape what she regards as worse than death—companionship with a brutal tyrant. Many a sad story of disappointed hopes and cruel sufferings are unwritten in China as well as in our own country.

The Chinese law recognizes the right of the parents to govern their children, and gives them authority in all matters pertaining to family government. At the same time it protects the children from neglect and cruelty on the part of their parents. Much is naturally and wisely left to parental affection. Any parent, who is not a brute, desires to see his children happy, to see them prepared for an honorable position in society, and therefore treats them kindly, educates them as far as he can, and encourages them to be virtuous and industrious.

The birth of a son is always hailed with joy in a Chinese home, but the birth of a daughter is regarded as a misfortune, and the little stranger is treated with neglect. Thousands are cast out to perish. I have frequently, during my residence in China, seen infant children lying out in the open fields, wrapped in pieces of matting or other material. There is just outside of the city wall, at Shanghai, a tower, known as the "baby tower," into which children are thrown. I do not know that infants are ever thrown into it alive, but I do know that it was used as a depository for dead children. Nor do I know that the infants exposed in the fields were cast out alive, but I know that such was my impression. It may be that they were the children of the poor, who did not feel able to bury their dead. That infanticide exists in China there can be no question, but to what extent is a matter of doubt. It is always confined to *female* children.

When a son is born one of the first things his parents do is to give him his first or "milk name," which he retains until he enters school, when he receives his "school name." On the day appointed for the ceremony the mother worships the Goddess of Mercy, and the boy, having his head shaved, is brought into the presence of friends, where the father confers the name and celebrates the occasion with a feast. No such honor is ever conferred on the despised girl. She may go nameless, or receive, instead of a name, a depreciating epithet. When a man marries he adopts a third name, by which he is usually known through life. If appointed to office he assumes an "official name," by which he is known to government. The head of each commercial firm takes a business name, by which he is known in business circles; and old men of fifty, shopkeepers and others,

15

A BRIDAL PROCESSION.

take a "shop name," which appears on their signboards as the name of the shop. When a man dies he receives still another and last name in the "hall of ancestors." This multiplicity of names would seem to make the identity of the person a difficult matter.

### CONVENTIONAL ETIQUETTE.

The elaborate forms of social etiquette among the Chinese appear to a Western man exceedingly absurd, and are often made a subject of mirth. These forms have, however, a basis of good sense. They are a substitute for caste distinctions, such as exist in India. Men are honored according to their station in society and according to their age. The emperor, being, according to the genius of the Chinese government, the representative of heaven, demands the same form of homage from his subjects that is observed in the worship of the gods. The court etiquette is therefore in character a form of religious worship, by which the universal supremacy of the emperor is recognized. It is a ritual, and should be so understood. All the officers of the empire are his representatives, and are therefore entitled to recognition as such; and as the Chinese are conquered subjects, having been subdued by the Manchoo Tartars, their allegiance to the ruling dynasty must also be recognized in all official intercourse; hence the importance of observing strictly "the rites" ordained by the government.

There are eight gradations in the ceremonial

etiquette. The first is the common salutation among equals and friends, such as you see on the streets, in tea shops, etc. It is merely joining your own hands and raising them before the breast, with a slight inclination of the head. The second is a low bow, with the hands thus clasped. The third, bending the knee, as if about to kneel. The fourth, actual kneeling. The fifth, kneeling and striking the head on the ground. Sixth, kneeling and knocking the head three times on the ground. Seventh, kneeling and striking the head three times on the ground, then standing upright and again kneeling and striking the head three times on the ground. The last and highest is kneeling three times and knocking the head nine times on the ground, or " three times three." This is considered by the government as the highest expression of loyalty to the ruling dynasty, and was the form demanded of the representatives of foreign governments a few years ago, but never submitted to by any Western power having any self-respect. I do not know that the representatives of any nation, not tributary to China, ever degraded themselves by such an act. The arrogance and insolence of the Chinese have been reduced to a decent respect for other nations, at least so far as official etiquette is concerned. The hated foreign barbarian has walked at pleasure through the imperial courts, and dictated to the haughty Manchoo autocrat the conditions of peace and the terms of treaties.

Enough, perhaps, has been said of the official etiquette of the Chinese government. Such matters are not especially interesting to the common reader.

The children of the family, among the better class of Chinese, are carefully instructed in domestic and social manners. There are first the relations of the several members of the family—father and mother, elder and junior sons, and the daughters and domestics. There is a manual of manners, called the Book of Rites, which contains full instructions as to the duties growing out of the family relations. As heretofore stated, the parents, especially the fathers, are given absolute control over domestic life in the home, except in matters regulated by law or general custom. The observance of the rules laid down in the Book of Rites depends, of course, upon the degree of education and social culture in the parents. To quote the Book of Rites therefore is not to say what is the actual character of the home life of the average Chinese family, but what it should be according to the "rites." The inner domestic life of the Chinese has not been observed by foreigners with sufficient minuteness to enable anyone to speak with accuracy. My own observation was limited to a casual view into the domestic arrangements of a few homes of the lower and middle classes.

Social life among the people of China is more public, and comes under the eye of the stranger more frequently and to an extent that the domestic life does not, and we consequently know much more about it. The following description of a social visit, from the pen of a friend who has enjoyed exceptional opportunities to observe Chinese social etiquette, is full and accurate:

"A Chinese gentleman in visiting his friend goes in a sedan chair. As he approaches the house he takes out his card—a large slip of red paper on which his name is written—and sends it in by the doorkeeper, who carries it to his master. If his friend is at home, the sedan is carried into the doorway, where the host meets him. The guest steps out of the sedan, each one advancing just so far, bowing just so many times, going through the regulation ceremony, which both parties understand, until they have reached the head of the hall, where they are seated, the guest sitting on the left hand, the place of honor in China. Tea and pipes are always presented. If the guest inquire after the health of the family, he is expected to begin with the oldest member; then the boys are inquired after. It is not good manners to ask about the wife, or to mention her in any way. If she is mentioned at all by her husband, it is as 'the stupid one of the inner chamber.' The children are called 'pigs' and 'puppies.' A child calls his father 'the majesty of the family,' or 'prince of the home,' etc. When inquiring after a father or grandfather, the guest is expected to say, 'Does the venerable great man enjoy happiness?' That is, How is your father's health? And so through the catalogue of persons and things about which it is proper to speak. Of course, among relatives or intimate friends, this stilted etiquette is omitted, or modified so as to relieve its stiffness and formality."

Private meals and public feasts among the higher classes are exceedingly formal. No ladies are ever present. An invitation to dinner is written on a slip of red paper like a visiting card, and sent some days before the time appointed. Another card is sent on the day itself, stating the hour of dinner, or a servant comes to call the guests, as in the parable. (Matt. xxii. 3, 4.) The host, dressed in his cap and robes, awaits the arrival of his guests. After they are all assembled, he invites them to lay aside their dresses of ceremony. They are then conducted into the dining room, and are seated by the host according to age or rank in twos on each side of small uncovered tables, and here the feast is served by well-trained domestics—all males, of course. The succession of dishes is not uniform, and the whole feast is regulated more by local custom than by any fixed general rules; yet there is such a sameness in the dishes and manner of serving them, in all parts of the empire, that a stranger would not perceive the slight variations which mark the custom in different localities. Usually the whole order seems to be the reverse of that to which we are accustomed. The desserts, sweetmeats, etc., are served first; then a variety of small dishes, sometimes numbering as many as forty, ending with soup. Among the peculiar articles of diet exhibited at a Chinese feast are shark's fins, bird's-nest soup, and pigeon eggs preserved in lime. I remember tasting an egg said to be five years old! A more disgusting morsel I never put into my mouth before nor since. I imagine now sometimes that I can almost taste the abominable thing. The Chinese use a native wine at their feasts, but seldom drink to excess.

CITY WALL AND CANAL.

## CHAPTER XX.

### Festivals and Amusements.

THE principal festivals observed by the Chinese are *New Year*, *Ching Ming*—or worshiping at the tombs*—the *Two Solstices*, and the festival of *Dragon Boats*. The New Year is a season of universal festivity. Its approach is heralded by great preparations in every place throughout the land. In the cities, on all the main streets, curious and costly articles are exposed for sale, sometimes as a mere business speculation, and in many instances as a matter of necessity, in order to procure money for the approaching festivities. It is customary to make presents to employees at this happy season; shopmen send presents to their customers as an acknowledgment of indebtedness for the business favors of the past year; friends also exchange tokens. Just before New Year there is a "general cleaning," washing, scouring, etc.; so that even in China they have some ideas of cleanliness, at least of external cleanliness, once a year.

New Year is general "pay day" in China, and anyone who would maintain a respectable standing as an honest or safe business man must be able to settle with all his creditors in a satisfactory manner. It is a busy day with shopkeepers,

---
* See "Ancestral Worship"—Williams, Davis, etc.

who may be seen going to and fro at all hours of the day, and even through the night; for by an innocent little fiction it is considered daylight with the creditor seeking his debtor as long as there is light; and when the sun has ceased to give the light, the creditor takes his lantern and thus furnishes his own light and pursues the debtor until he gets his money or loses his case. This custom of yearly settlements saves many a man from bankruptcy, avoids lawsuits, and prevents misunderstandings in the settlement of accounts. The relatives of a man in business are held to certain responsibilities for his debts; so that if he seems disposed to contract obligations beyond his means to meet them, they can give notice to his creditors, and he is forced to make an assignment or exhibit assets sufficient to satisfy all parties. The usages to which I have referred may not be common in all parts of the empire, but that New-year's day is general "pay day" throughout the land I think is true.\*

In some places the family sit down to a substantial supper on New-year's eve with a pan of charcoal under the table as a supposed preventive against fires. After the supper is ended the wooden lamp-stools are brought out and spread upon the pavement with a pile of gold and silver paper, which is set on fire after all the demons have been warned off by a volley of firecrackers. The embers are then divided into twelve heaps, and

---

\* See "Middle Kingdom."

their manner of going out carefully watched as a prognostic of the kind of weather to be expected during the ensuing year. Other superstitious ceremonies peculiar to the locality are observed by individuals and families.

Devout persons are as careful to settle with the gods as with their human creditors at this season. A few days before the new year the temples are crowded with worshipers, both men and women, rich and poor. Some fast and engage the priests to pray for them that their sins may be forgiven, and that they may be able to enter upon the new year with a clean record. Many ornament their houses by pasting papers upon the doors and walls, signifying their desire that " The Five Blessings," which contain the sum of all human felicity, may abide with them during the year. These blessings are " longevity, riches, health, love of virtue, and a natural death." These papers are pasted on every boat, every oar, on bow and stern, and every available place about all classes and sizes of boats. They are placed on farmhouses, on trees, on boards, posts, etc. The constant explosion of firecrackers and the beating of gongs make day and night hideous. The demons of discord and strife, and all that have evil intentions toward men or their families, are supposed to be frightened far away by this horrible uproar. New-year's day is also a great occasion for jugglers, actors, and mountebanks of all kinds.

*The Feast of Dragon Boats* occurs on the fifth

day of the fifth month, and is a lively festival. Pairs of long, narrow boats, holding sixty or more rowers, race up and down the rivers, making a great clamor, as if searching for some one who had been drowned. This festival was instituted about B.C. 300, in memory of a statesman who drowned himself in the Yang-tse-Kiang. Search was made for his body by the people, who loved him for his virtues, and this mode of remembering him has been continued ever since. The bow of the boat is ornamented with the dragon's head, and the men beat gongs and drums and wave flags.

*The Feast of Lanterns*, which takes place at the first full moon in each year, is a dull and uninteresting festival. How it originated is unknown. It is known, however, to have been observed since A.D. 700.

There are other festivals celebrated annually by this singular people, but none that would be especially interesting to my young readers. (See chapter on "Agriculture"—emperor plowing, etc.)

### AMUSEMENTS OF THE CHINESE.

The Chinese have a childish fondness for shows and public parades of all kinds. They are also fond of games, especially games of chance. They are devoted to gambling. A boy prefers to risk his own cash on the cast of a die to simply buying a cake without trying the chance of getting it for nothing. Gaming houses are opened by scores. Tables with the implements of gambling stand at almost every street corner, and in every public place. It is said that the women in the privacy of their homes are devoted to cards and dominoes; and everybody who has been in a Chinese city knows how universal certain forms of gambling are. "Cricket fighting" is a common Chinese amusement. Two crickets are put into a basin, and teased with a straw till they rush at each other in the utmost fury, crying in a sharp and angry tone as they engage in the fight. Cash (money) is staked upon the result of the battle by the bystanders. Usually one of the combatants loses a limb, sometimes his life, in the fierce conflict. Little cages, made of bamboo, silver, and sometimes of gold, are used by rich young men to carry their game crickets. Quails are also trained to fight, like chicken cocks in this country. Such is the mania for betting that a number of gentlemen sitting at a tea table will stake their money on the direction in which a certain fly will go when it takes wing. One man will perhaps say "west;" another will say "south;" another, "east," etc. The fly must not be disturbed, but left to follow its own impulses.

The flying of paper kites is a favorite amusement of men as well as children. The old man seventy years of age is seen seated on the city wall, or some other elevated position, flying his "butterfly kite" with as much apparent pleasure as the ten-year-old boy that sits near him with his long "centipede kite." I have seen kites of the latter shape one hundred feet in length, writhing and squirming in the air at a great height. It requires much skill to fly certain kinds of kites. Some of the more common forms have a light bamboo bow, with a silk cord or bow string attached to them in such manner as to imitate a coarse Æolian harp in sound. It is not unpleasant to hear a number of these harps singing in the upper air. I know of nothing among the Chinese more characteristic of their social manners than the simplicity of their amusements. They are children in this matter—easily amused. They have never been fond of gladiatorial sports, or of any form of violent or dangerous exercise. Fighting among themselves seldom occurs. When two persons fall out, instead of pounding each other, or seeking to take each other's lives, they enter into a stormy and wordy discussion, in which opprobrious epithets are freely exchanged. They seem to be greatly excited, scream at the top of their voices, gesticulate violently, rush toward each other until their noses almost touch, and then retreat and take breath, to repeat the same violent and absurd performance. However terrible their threats or alarming their gestures, they seldom touch each other. Duels are unknown, and assassinations infrequent. It is said that where a dispute becomes so serious that blood must be shed, one of the parties takes his own life instead of his enemy's, and thus becomes a malignant ghost with greatly increased powers to avenge himself on his adversary. The one who survives is stigmatized by his neighbors as a murderer, one whose cruel treatment has driven a fellow-man out of the world. The living man can do his enemy no more harm, while the ghost of the dead man has superhuman powers of evil, and can torment his enemy at will; he can destroy his property, life, happiness, and everything good belonging to him.

Among the persons employed to entertain private parties, or the general public, none is more popular than the professional juggler. He is seen everywhere—in the homes of the rich, on the public square, in the vicinity of temples, in villages, hamlets, and country places. Some of his "tricks" are wonderful. In the public square at Shanghai I have frequently seen an old juggler perform. One of his most popular feats was to take a Chinese dinner—with all the furniture for a small table, chopsticks, plates, cups, spoons, etc., and all the food—out of an empty tea pot. Of course I knew that it was all sleight of hand, but it was so cleverly done that I sometimes felt almost sure that it was a reality. This performance is one common among Chinese jugglers, and is not considered specially wonderful. The Japanese and Hindoo jugglers are said to be much more expert than the Chinese.

"Theatrical entertainments are very common among the Chinese, and when public are usually connected with some religious festival in honor of the god before whose temple they are exhibited. They are generally gotten up by the priests, who send their neophytes around with a subscription paper, and then engage as large and skillful a band of performers as their funds will allow. Parties of actors and tumblers are numerous, and can be had cheaply, and their performances frequently relieve the tedium of private life of rich families who engage them to come to their houses. The rich sometimes erect private theaters and employ actors to perform for the amusement of the family and friends. The scenery of a Chinese theater is very simple, consisting merely of painted mats arranged on the back and sides of the stage, a few tables, chairs, or beds, which successively serve for many purposes, and are brought in and out of the robing room. The orchestra is seated on the side of the stage. The dresses are made of gorgeous silks, and present the best specimen of ancient Chinese costumes now to be seen."* The following description of a play, witnessed by a foreigner several years ago, will give the reader some idea of the Chinese drama: "The first scene was intended to represent the happiness and splendor of beings who inhabit the upper regions, with the sun and moon, and the elements curiously personified, playing around them. The man who personated the sun held a round image of the sun's disk, while the female who acted the part of the moon had a crescent in her hand. The actors took care to move so as to imitate the conjunctions and oppositions of the heavenly bodies as they move

---

* Dr. Williams.

around in their apparent orbits. The thunderer wielded an ax, and leaped and dashed about in a variety of extraordinary somersaults. After a few turns the monarch who had been so highly honored as to find a place, through the partiality of a mountain nymph, in the abodes of the happy, begins to feel that no height of good fortune can secure a mortal against the common calamities of this frail life. A wicked courtier disguises himself in a tiger's skin, and in this garb imitates the fierce animal in his actions. He rushes into the apartments of the ladies, frightens them out of their wits, and throws the heir apparent into the moat. The sisters hurry into the royal presence, and, casting themselves on the ground, divulge the sad intelligence that a tiger has carried off the prince, who, it appears, was the son of the mountain nymph who had befriended the monarch. The loss of his son so affects the monarch that he abdicates his throne, and through the intrigues of an artful woman selects a fool as his successor. The king dies, the fool is frightened at his position, and the artful woman has things her own way. The state is plunged into civil discord at home and dangerous wars abroad."

An English writer who was for many years a resident in China, and who studied the social life of the people with great care, says of the Chinese stage that "the morals of the pieces exhibited in their theaters are better than the acting which is sometimes seen in the West. No indecent exposure of the person is ever seen, such as ballet dancers, etc. The female characters are assumed by men and boys. The audience stand in front of the stage; it may be in the hot sun. The police are always on hand to preserve order, but their services are seldom required, for the Chinese are a peaceable and order-loving people."

The more manly and active sports, such as bowling alley, cricket match, rowing, or any of the athletic games of the West, are not popular with the Chinese; they prefer to exhibit their strength and skill in lifting heavy weights, hurling large stones, and such like exercises.

The amusements of the Chinese which I witnessed were only such as are exhibited out of doors. I never entered any of the "dens," except an opium shop, and that only once. I never was in a theater at home or abroad, and saw the Chinese plays only because they were performed openly on the street, like the tricks of the jugglers.

### OPIUM SMOKING.

It may seem a little out of logical order to class "opium smoking" with Chinese amusements; but I do not see a more appropriate place for it. It is regarded by its devotees as one of the greatest pleasures of life until the third stage of experience has been reached, and the victim enters the "regions of the lost."

Opium smoking in China is the national form of intemperance, and is one of the most debauching and ruinous vices ever practiced by any people.

Dr. Smith, of Penang, who had every opportunity to observe and study the subject, says: "The baleful effects of this habit on the human constitution are particularly displayed by stupor, forgetfulness, general deterioration of all the mental faculties, emaciation, debility, sallow complexion, lividness of the lips and eyelids, languor and lack-luster of eye, and appetite either destroyed or depraved." Another writer says: "It exhausts the animal spirits, impedes the regular performance of business, wastes the flesh and blood, dissipates every kind of property, renders the person ill-favored, promotes obscenity, discloses secrets, violates the laws, attacks the vitals, and ends in a horrible death." Dr. Williams, speaking of the habit, says: "The thirst and burning sensation in the throat which the wretched sufferer feels, only to be removed by a repetition of the dose, proves one of the strongest links in his chain. At this stage of the habit his case is almost hopeless. If the pipe be delayed too long, vertigo, complete prostration, and discharge of water from the eyes ensue; if entirely withheld, coldness and aching pains are felt over the body, and death soon closes the scene."

Suicide is often committed in China by swallowing opium. A woman becomes angry at her husband, or is displeased with her parents, and takes opium, and unless relieved is soon dead. Opium imparts no benefit to the smoker, but injures his health, beclouds his mind, and unfits him for any useful occupation. One of the greatest difficulties with which the Christian missionary has to contend in China is the almost universal habit of opium smoking. I remember that while I was in China an effort was made by the missionaries to ascertain what proportion of the male population of China was addicted to the habit, and my recollection is that the proportion was supposed to be eight out of every ten! After a Chinaman has contracted the habit there is little hope that he will ever reform. Of the few apostates among native Christians, the majority, it is said, had been opium smokers. On the contrary, reformed smokers, cured by God's grace, are among the most sincere and active believers in the native Church.

I shall not attempt to describe the manner of preparing and smoking this poisonous drug. It is, like drinking whisky, a disgusting and demoralizing sight. A madhouse is a more cheerful place than an opium den. Indeed, nothing can be more revolting than one of these "Chinese hells." Yet, besotted by opium as China is, the blessed gospel has power to heal and to save its millions.

PUNISHMENT IN SCHOOL.

## CHAPTER XXI.

### Superstitions of the Chinese.

THE Chinese are Asiatics, and as such given to superstition. Some one has said that "God committed to the four great nations of history the education of the human race. To the Jews was assigned the training of the conscience, or moral sense, of mankind; to the Asiatics, the imagination; to the Greeks, the æsthetic faculties; and to the Romans, the development of the will power."\* However this may be, we find these peculiar characteristics predominant in the four great races. To the Jews God delivered the moral law, and made them the custodians of revealed truth, so that "salvation is of the Jews." The Hindoos have cultivated the imagination. They have reveled in mysticism, religious fanaticism, and in all forms of metaphysical speculation. Most of the heresies that have disturbed the peace of the religious and philosophical world have had their origin in Asia. Even the stolid and practical Chinese have given evidence of their Asiatic birth in their fondness for the fantastic superstitions that disfigure all their systems of belief.

Not content with three systems of religion—Buddhism, Confucianism, and Taoism—they have

---

\* Draper's "Intellectual Development of Europe."

"gods many" besides those belonging to these systems. Among those most generally worshiped by the people, without respect to any religious sect, are heaven and earth.* These are supposed to be the authors of all things, "the father and mother of men and things," and are therefore objects of worship. This worship is usually performed without the intervention of the priests—a sort of domestic service. In some families it is performed night and morning; with others, only on special occasions. The father of the family usually performs the ceremony. He takes a bunch of incense in his hand and stands in the door of his house. When the smoke of the incense begins to rise, he bows reverently toward the earth and repeats a short prayer.

In some parts of the empire the farmer, or the carpenter, before breaking the soil for sowing grain, building a house, or digging a well, gives formal notice to the earth, asking pardon for disfiguring or wounding the face of the dear "mother," declaring that he would not dare to do so were it not an absolute necessity. Sometimes a priest is called in to read prayers and otherwise conciliate the *local deity* that presides over the ground to be disturbed by the proposed labor.

There are many other occasions when it is thought necessary to propitiate the earth by certain religious ceremonies. It is often difficult to ascertain what the devotee means by the rites he

---

*Culbertson: "Religions of China."

performs. If you ask him he will probably answer, "Custom;" and there the information ends.

*The God of the Kitchen* is an object of universal reverence; or, perhaps I should rather say, of universal fear. No family would feel safe without a shrine for this god over the cooking range; and yet he is regarded not as a friend and patron, but as an uncanny spy, who sees and knows all that takes place in the house during the year, and who makes an annual report to the powers above, "naught concealing" or "covering over with friendly gloss." The image of this god is not made of wood or stone, but is simply a broad strip of paper on which the uncouth features of the deity are printed. His term of office expires with the end of the year, when he is sent off in flames to the regions above, and his successor—a new paper image—is installed with due ceremonies, and another year of espionage begins.

*The Rain Dragon* is another creature of the imagination to which the Chinese render homage. They believe that there is a great dragon somewhere above the earth, in the region of the clouds, that gives or withholds rain at his will. If he is offended by the sins of the people, especially by the unfaithfulness of the rulers, there is no rain. If the drought be long continued, and a famine be probable, there is great alarm throughout the threatened district, and the people look to their rulers for relief. One of the measures adopted by the magistrates is a proclamation forbidding the slaughter of animals. They first forbid the slaughter of the larger animals; but if the drought be continued, the prohibition extends to poultry, and even to fish. This prohibition is not to enforce a general fast, but to show respect for the Buddhist doctrine which forbids the taking of life. Meat that has already been slaughtered may be eaten in any quantity. There is no intention on the part of the people to exercise self-denial.

If rain does not follow the arrest of the slaughter of animals, then other measures are resorted to, such as processions in which a great image of the dragon is conspicuous. The magistrates appear in the processions with signs of mourning upon their persons. They visit the temples where they prostrate themselves, offer prayers, with confession of sin, not only on their own behalf but as the official representatives of the people. Sometimes, in seasons of great distress because of the drought, the idols in the temples are brought out of their cool retreats and exposed in the sun, that they may know how hot and dry it is. I witnessed a scene like this in the city of Shanghai, China, in 1856, during a season of protracted drought. The magistrates said the gods seemed to be indifferent to the miseries of the people, and did not believe that the land was burning up under a rainless sky. They were therefore dragged out of the temples and placed in the public square, where they could feel the full force of the sun's heat. After a time rain fell, and the people believed it was because the gods were made to realize the true condition of things! The Rain Dragon is worshiped only when his help is needed. In ordinary circumstances he is entirely neglected.

*The God of Thunder* is one of the deities which the Chinese worship on occasions when he manifests himself in the thunder storm or tempest. They are greatly alarmed when they hear his awful voice, as they believe, "tearing the clouds of heaven asunder." Many observe a fast on the day in which they hear thunder. It is a common belief among the people that no one is ever struck by lightning who has not committed some crime for which the law has not or cannot punish him. They say, however, that this god has a great dislike for snakes, and that it may happen sometimes, when he is hurling his bolts at a serpent concealed under a house, that he may strike one of the inmates; but this is purely an accident, and an exception to the rule. The image of this god is an enormous creature, resembling a huge giant with many fantastic additions. With one hand he beats a great drum, and in the other he holds a number of thunderbolts. He is a fearful monster in appearance.

*The God of Fire* is an object of special fear. Large temples are erected to him, and at the vernal equinox and winter solstice he is worshiped with expensive ceremonies. Business men give liberally to the support of this god, as men in our country give to insurance companies, to protect themselves against loss by fire. On one occasion at Shanghai, in 1855, a fire broke out in the business portion of the city and fifty thousand dollars' worth of property was destroyed. Those who had property in the vicinity of the fire, but which escaped destruction, spent some two hundred dollars in thank offerings as an expression of their gratitude to the God of Fire for protecting their property. It so happened, however, that another fire visited the neighborhood some weeks afterwards, and the property of the men who had made the thank offering was consumed. This greatly enraged them, and they vowed that they would never worship the God of Fire again. During the fire the shrine of the principal deity in the neighborhood was consumed and his godship perished in the flames! One would think that such proofs of the folly of trusting in idols would drive the people away from their altars. But where should they go? They do not know the true God. Besides, "they are mad upon their idols."

*Calling Back the Spirit.*—The Chinese, no matter where they die, are anxious to be buried in their native soil; not because they love their own country so much, but because they desire to lie where their descendants can visit their tombs and perform the "ancestral rites," without which their spirits would have neither friends, food, nor clothing in the next world. With no one to worship at their tombs, they would be of all the spirits in hades the most miserable. This is the reason why so many bodies of Chinese are sent from California back to China for burial.

When a Chinese dies abroad, his body is always carried to his native place, if the family can bear the expense. But it would be a sad thing if the spirit should be unable or unwilling to accompany the body; they have therefore a ceremony by which the spirit is persuaded to return and remain with the body. If one is lost at sea, the friends go as near as possible to the place where he was lost, and call back the spirit. Sometimes immediately after the breath leaves the body of one who dies at home, a member of the family takes some part of the deceased's wearing apparel, and going to the door calls in tender, pleading tones to the spirit to come back. If the person supposed to be dead should revive, the friends believe that the spirit heard the call and returned to the body. The priests are frequently employed to assist in the ceremony.

When a child dies under sixteen years of age, quite a different performance takes place, one that nothing less cruel than heathenism could tolerate. This is called "sweeping away the spirit." The object is to frighten away the spirit of the child, that it may not trouble the family. This unnatural and foolish conceit is based on the belief that the child suffered an injury or wrong from one of the parents, in a former state of existence, and that it was sent into the family to avenge the wrong. They wish, therefore, so thoroughly to frighten its little ghost by firing crackers and beating drums that it will never venture to return. When a child dies in a Chinese family there is no lamentation, no weeping or wailing, as when a grown person dies. No special care is taken of its little body. It is treated in all respects as a mere "thing"—classed with the lower animals. There are, however, mothers in China, in whom the natural maternal instinct is too strong to be crushed out by even the heartless teachings of heathenism—they love their children. In some places, where two children, betrothed by their parents, die before the marriage ceremony is performed, their spirits are married. The tablets of the children are used as representatives of the little ones, and they are married in due form. Sometimes the parents of dead children enter into marriage contracts for the deceased babies, and their spirits are supposed to be united in the spirit world!

Nearly all the Chinese superstitions are in some way connected with the spirits of the dead, and it may be said truly, I think, that they are " in bondage through fear " of ghosts all their lives. They believe the air to be full of spirits, that they are going to and fro night and day; and what seems strange, they fear the spirits of their dead friends seemingly as much as any others. All disembodied spirits are supposed to be malignant, and to possess great power to harm men in the flesh. I have perhaps furnished enough examples of popular superstitions for the present purpose. I will, however, give some of a different character illustrating the Chinese ideas of astrology, lucky and unlucky days, etc.*

*Worship of the Stars.*—Astrology has been a subject of study in China from a very early day. Many of the stars are worshiped. Temples are erected to the "Seven Precious Ones;" that is, the seven principal stars in the "Great Bear." The God of Literature is supposed to reside in one of the stars in this constellation. The "Great Dipper" is an object of veneration; it is supposed to possess great influence over the fortunes of men, and is the guardian of the official residences of China. The five planets—Mercury, Venus, Mars, Jupiter, and Saturn—rule over the year and the four seasons. These planets are also connected with the twelve signs of the zodiac. These signs are represented by twelve animals—the rat, cow, tiger, rabbit, dragon, snake, horse, sheep, monkey, cock, dog, and bear. The influence of the planets, combined with other occult forces, controls the destinies of individuals and nations, and constitutes the heathen providence that governs the world. The priest, or diviner, casts the horoscope for the year, and then for every day, hour, and moment of time. In one year all central places will be lucky, another year unlucky; sometimes the north, sometimes the south, east, or west. Certain days will be lucky, and certain

---

* For much that I have said in regard to the superstitions of the Chinese, I am indebted to Drs. Culbertson, Morrison, Maclay, and others.

other days unlucky. It is the duty of the Astronomical Board, at Peking, to ascertain beforehand the peculiar character of each day in the year, and report it in the Imperial Almanac. Thus every act of life is supposed to be dependent upon these ever-changing influences. The whole Chinese people live and die under bondage to the grossest superstitions. There are a few wise men, however, among the many millions of China, who do not believe in these foolish vagaries, but the number is small. The devil is a cruel master. There is no joy, peace, or hope in his service; all is sorrow, darkness, despair, and death.

*Table Turning.*—The Chinese, long before such a thing was thought of in Europe or America, were consulting spirits in the other world by "mediums," "spirit writing," "table turning," etc. The "medium" is a sorceress by profession, and is supposed to be able to do wonderful things by the aid of her patron demon. She is feared, and her services are often invoked to ward off some threatened evil, or to conciliate some malignant spirit that is supposed to be troubling the family. These superstitious beliefs and ceremonies, like many other customs of the Chinese, differ widely in different localities; and it is important for the reader to remember this fact, for he will see contradictory statements in regard to many of the peculiar usages of different provinces.

The Chinese believe that not only the spirits of men, but the ghosts of animals, are able to give information through the "spirit medium." Some years ago (1852), Dr. Culbertson says, a "Taoist priest professed to be in communication with the spirit of an old fox, which had lived thousands of years ago. The fox had become a young lady, and would converse through the priest with persons who wished to know the best means of promoting their worldly interests." The priest was probably a ventriloquist.

The process of "table turning" is generally about as follows, with some local variations: The table is turned upside down upon a pair of chopsticks laid at right angles over the mouth of a bowl filled with water. Four persons lay one hand on each leg of the table, while with the free hand each grasps one hand of his neighbor, thus forming "a circle." A prayer is now chanted by the "medium," and soon the table begins to move. The persons forming the "circle" move with it, and in a few minutes it is whirling rapidly upon its axis, until it is thrown off its balance on the floor. This is the "table-turning mystery." The "medium" may have communication with the spirits orally, but usually the ghosts prefer to write their messages, and the table is thus generally brought into use. The table is covered with sand or flour. Then a small basket without a handle is armed with a pencil or chopstick tied to its side. The basket is then turned upside down, its edges resting upon the tips of one or two fingers of two persons standing on opposite sides of the table in such manner that the pencil touches the surface of the table. After a short time the basket begins to move, and traces the characters, which any literary person can read. And thus the message from the spirit is communicated to the medium, often on subjects of which the operators know nothing. Sometimes the spirit invoked cannot write, then nothing can be done.

Charms and amulets of various kinds are employed to ward off evil influences, to drive away malignant spirits, and to cure diseases. In case of sickness, spells—consisting of mystical characters written on paper—are burned, and the patient drinks the ashes in tea. Sometimes the poor, when suffering with extreme hunger, resort to a similar charm to drive away the pangs of starvation. Mothers use amulets to protect their children from evil spirits, bad luck, sickness, etc. The "eight diagrams" are generally employed for this purpose. They are engraved on a copper disk and suspended by a silk cord around the neck of the child. The Chinese believe that the evil spirits which infest the home have a great antipathy to red, and that a piece of red cloth worn on the person will drive them away. In addition to this precaution, some families purchase the figure of a white tiger, an imaginary creature whose power they fear. A piece of meat is suspended from the tongue of this paper monster, which he is supposed to eat. The whole affair is then burned, and the danger from this source averted.

Tall pagodas are erected in the vicinity of cities for protection against evil influences. The celebrated porcelain tower at Nanking was erected for this purpose. It was a wonderful structure, built by the third emperor of the Ming dynasty, about A.D. 1413. It was two hundred and sixty feet high, and three hundred feet in circumference at the base. It was built of porcelain beautifully glazed, and of various colors. The most prominent color was green, mingled with red, yellow, and white. It was destroyed by the Taiping insurgents in 1855, one of the most outrageous pieces of vandalism on record in the history of the world. Of course it had no value as a protection against evil influences, but it was justly classed with the wonders of human labor and skill.

The Rev. Arthur H. Smith, in his "Chinese Characteristics," says: "It has often been remarked, and with every appearance of truth, that there is no other civilized nation in existence which is under such bondage to superstition and credulity as the Chinese. Wealthy merchants and learned scholars are not ashamed to be seen, on the two days of the month set apart for the purpose, worshiping the fox, the weasel, the hedgehog, the snake, and the rat, all of which are printed on placards, styled 'Their Excellencies,' and are thought to have an important effect on human destiny." Could anything be more absurd or ridiculous than a high official, in his robes of office, on his knees knocking his head on the ground before the image of a rat, and addressing the miserable little creature as "Your Excellency;" or worshiping a hedgehog with the same ceremony? Mr. Smith says: "Not many years ago a prominent statesman fell on his knees before a water-snake which some one had been pleased to represent as the embodiment of the God of Floods, supposed to be the incarnation of an official of a former dynasty, whose success with brimming rivers was supposed to be marvelous."

### PECULIARITIES OF THE CHINESE.

The eccentricities of Chinese character and conduct have become proverbial throughout the civilized world. It is a common remark among Europeans that if you wish to know how the Chinese would do a certain thing, consider how you would do it, and then reverse the process. Their national isolation and the inordinate self-conceit of the race have led to the development of many singular characteristics which distinguish them as the most unique and peculiar people in the world. Their absurd veneration of the past has kept them stationary in thought for centuries. Nothing is too absurd to command respect, provided it belongs to an early antiquity. Mistakes in their classics have been carefully perpetuated generation after generation, because found in some ancient copies. The Chinese have "the habit of announcing as a reason for a fact the fact itself. 'Why do you not put salt into your bread cakes?' you ask a Chinese cook. 'We do not put salt into our bread cakes,' is the explanation. 'How is it with so much and such beautiful ice in your city none of it is stored up for summer?' 'No. We do not store up ice for summer,' is the answer."*

The following list of eccentric variations from what we regard as right and proper may suffice to illustrate what is usually meant by "Chinese peculiarities:"

The place of honor among the Chinese is on the left hand, and not on the right hand as with us.

The Chinaman shakes his own hands, and not the hand of his friend when greeting him.

The Chinese magnetic needle points to the south, and not to the north.

The Chinaman sleeps with his head on a block of wood, or on a brick, instead of resting it on a pillow.

The Chinese carpenter pulls his plane toward himself, instead of pushing it from him. He also pulls his saw, instead of pushing it as we do.

The tailor pushes his needle from him in sewing; and instead of putting his "goose" in the fire to heat it, he puts the fire in the goose.

The Chinaman begins to read at the end of the book, or on the right hand, and not at the left hand as we do; and he reads from top to bottom of the page, and not from left to right.

He begins his dinner with the dessert, and ends with the soup.

He scratches his foot when puzzled, and not his

---

*Smith: "Chinese Characteristics."

head; laughs when his friends die, or when relating bad news, and weeps over trifles.

When one Chinaman sends a present to his friend, he expects one in return of equivalent value. He will offer you his house and all it contains as a free gift, with the understanding that he means no more than when he asks you to take a seat. He does not mean for you to carry away the chair when you leave.

The Chinese never uncover the head in presence of company; it is considered an act of unbecoming familiarity.

A husband never speaks of loving his wife any more than a European would speak of loving his wife's servant maid. To inquire after the health of a man's wife, or of anything concerning her, is considered not merely an act of rudeness, but a serious offense.

The gift of a coffin or a burial suit of clothes is considered an appropriate expression of filial piety on the part of children. Every Chinaman desires to see his burial outfit before he dies.

The average Chinaman seems to see no more moral wrong in a lie than the Englishman does in a pun. It is simply amusing.

The Chinese have no pockets in their clothes. The sleeves of the outer garment serve the purpose of pockets.

They do not use feathers for beds, pillows, or clothing, but suffer them to be blown away by the wind, or decay in the back yards. It is strange that a people who appear to utilize everything else should neglect this.

A Chinese on being introduced to a stranger inquires first as to his honorable name, and secondly as to his honor's age.

On meeting of friends the salutation is, "Have you eaten rice?" The answer is always in the affirmative, though neither of the persons may have tasted food for twenty-four hours.

The Chinese never drink cold water, but slake their thirst with hot tea. They do not drink milk nor eat butter, and express great disgust for cheese. They may eat snails, slugs, and taste puppies, but will not touch cheese.

TRAVELING ON A WHEELBARROW.

The elderly woman on the right-hand seat of the wheelbarrow is MRS. QUAY, the celebrated "Bible Woman" of the Southern Methodist Mission, Shanghai, China.

## CHAPTER XXII.

### Christian Missions Among the Chinese.

TRADITION ascribes the first effort to convert the Chinese to Christianity to the apostle Thomas, but there is no authentic record to support the tradition. That the gospel was preached in China at a very early day, there is good reason to believe.*

*The Nestorian missionaries* arrived in China about the year 505. The only record of their labors is a tablet found in the province of Shen-See, in 1625, known as the " Nestorian monument." This tablet was erected in 788, and shows that Christianity had made great progress among the Chinese.

*The Roman Catholic Church* has had missions in China since 1288, when Monte Corvino was sent out by Pope Nicholas IV. to Tartary and China. He is reported to have been very successful, and the missions he founded continued to prosper until the expulsion of the Manchoos in 1368.

The second period of Romish missions in China includes a space of one hundred and fifty years, from the time that Matteo Ricci established himself at Canton in 1581 to 1736, when an edict

---

* See " Encyclopedia of Missions," Vol. I., p. 264. Also " Middle Kingdom," Vol. II., p. 290; Mosheim, etc.

was issued by the Emperor Yung-Ching sending all the missionaries out of the empire.

The edict of Yung-Ching marks another epoch in the history of Romish missions in China. From that day to the present time they have had a varied success in their work, sometimes in favor with the government and people, and sometimes sorely persecuted. They are still in the field, and claim a very large membership, but recent statistics show that they are decreasing in numbers and influence. The Romish Church in China has not only become grossly secular, but extensively paganized. It has compromised with the superstitions of heathenism, and sadly betrayed the cause of Christianity in China.

*Protestant missions* in China\* date from about the beginning of the present century. Dr. Robert Morrison, of the London Missionary Society, has the honor of being the first Protestant missionary to the Chinese. He was appointed in 1807, but was unable to obtain passage in an English ship, because the East India Company refused all missionaries passage in any of their ships, either to India or China. Dr. Morrison came to America and sailed from New York for Canton, China, in the ship "Trident," May 10, 1807. If England has the credit of appointing the first Protestant missionary to China, our country has the honor of furnishing him passage to his field of labor.†

---

\* Medhurst's "State and Prospects of China," Chap. X.; Life of Morrison, Vol. I.   † Morrison's Memoirs, Vol. I., p. 130.

The London Mission has done a good work in China. The men and women sent out have been deeply interested in their labors, and have manifested a high degree of intelligence and zeal. They have been very successful in making converts.

In 1829 the American Board of Commissioners for Foreign Missions sent the Rev. C. E. Bridgeman, the first American missionary to China, a man of ability, learning, and piety. He did a vast amount of valuable literary work. He founded, and conducted for many years, the *Chinese Repository*. I knew him well, and esteemed him greatly.

The American Baptist Missionary Union sent out the first missionary to the Chinese in 1833. He resided at first at Bangkok, in Siam, not being able to enter China.

In 1838 the American Presbyterian Board began its first missionary station at Singapore, and not in China, for the same reason that the Baptists began operations at Bangkok.

In 1842, at the close of the first opium war between England and China, five of the principal ports of China were opened to foreigners, and the island of Hong-Kong was ceded to the English. The country was thus made accessible to Christian missionaries, not only at the five ports, but indirectly to the inhabitants of the surrounding country. The Churches of Protestant Christendom immediately prepared to improve the new opportunities thus providentially afforded for work in China. Societies and laborers increased rapidly, and the opening of additional ports by the Tien-Tsin treaty still further enlarged their privileges and stimulated their zeal. There are now in China the representatives of nearly forty different missionary boards. A good degree of success has attended their efforts for the last several years, and the native churches are becoming more active and earnest in their efforts to propagate the gospel among their fellow-countrymen. Some of these churches are not only self-supporting, but contribute liberally to the cause of missions. The Bible societies of Europe and America, and the Bible and Tract Society of China, are doing a noble work.

According to the "Encyclopedia of Missions" (1891), there are now in China (or were in 1890) 1,295 missionaries; ordained natives, 209; unordained natives, 1,260; hospitals, 61; dispensaries, 43; patients, 348,439; organized churches, 520; wholly self-supporting, 94; communicants, 37,287; contributions of native Christians from 1876 to 1889, $36,884.54.

It does not come within the scope of this volume to give a detailed account of missionary work and its results in China. A brief sketch in outline is all that can be given. Books and periodicals can be procured almost anywhere from which full information in regard to the particulars of the work may be obtained. The average reader would not be specially interested in the details of the business

CHRISTIAN MISSIONS. 269

management of missionary boards and committees at home, or in the financial difficulties which limit and embarrass the laborers in the field; hence I omit them.

The Churches of America are represented in China by their agents, as follows: The American Board of Commissioners for Foreign Missions, 1829; American Protestant Episcopal, 1834; American Presbyterian (North), 1838; American Reformed, 1842; Methodist Episcopal Church, (North), 1847; Seventh Day Baptist, 1847; American Baptist (South), 1847; Methodist Episcopal Church (South), 1848; American Presbyterian (South), 1868; American Congregational, 1887.*

### WORK IN THE MISSION FIELD.

It may interest my youthful readers to have some account of what the missionaries in China do, and how they do it.

1. The first thing, of course, is the acquisition of the language. (For some account of the Chinese language the reader is referred to Chapter V.). The usual method is to employ a Chinese teacher (and he should be a man of some literary attainments). You take your seat with him at a table, and begin the laborious and discouraging task of learning one of the most difficult languages in the world. An old missionary said he believed the devil had invented the Chinese language to keep the people from becoming Christians. Like

---
* "Encyclopedia of Missions," 1891.

the people, it is *heathen*, and you have to deal with it accordingly.

You are at first practically deaf and dumb, for you can neither speak nor hear with any degree of intelligence. You place your hand on some object, perhaps a book, and look at your teacher. He gives you the Chinese name for it, which you repeat after him, imitating as nearly as you can the strange sounds which he utters; and so you proceed to learn the names of things. After you have learned the names of the principal objects in your room, you tackle simple phrases and sentences, such as the forms of salutation, the question, " What is this?" and thus acquire a vocabulary. There are " phrase books," prepared by foreigners for beginners, which aid in the process of learning the spoken language, and assist also in learning to read. You air your limited vocabulary with your servants and the people about you. Thus gradually, it may be very gradually, you acquire a knowledge of the language, and by and by you are able to deliver a short address, which in your complacency you may call a sermon, but it will be many months before you can really speak the language with sufficient fluency and clearness to be readily understood by the people generally. It is very discouraging, but " time, patience, and perseverance accomplish all things."

2. The next thing is to deliver your message. You have longed for the time when you could tell the heathen the wonderful story of God's love to

man; how "Christ Jesus came into the world to save sinners;" how he lived among men an ideal life of love, purity, and goodness; how he healed the sick, comforted the unfortunate, raised the dead, and opened up the way of life to a fallen and guilty race. You have desired most earnestly to tell them how the Saviour " suffered for us sinners and for our salvation;" how he was crucified; how he rose from the dead, and ascended to heaven where he now lives and reigns Lord of all. You have dreamed of leading some poor benighted and lost wanderers in the wilderness of heathenism to God and heaven.

### HINDRANCES TO MISSIONARY WORK.

But now that you are ready to enter upon the work in earnest, you find new difficulties and trials. You soon discover that the people for whose good you have left country, home, friends, and all you hold dear, despise you and your message. The rulers of the country hate Christianity bitterly, and the educated classes treat it and its teachers with lofty scorn. The common people call you a " foreign devil," and the official and literary classes characterize you as a " barbarian of low grade." You have perhaps imagined that the heathen were tired of the unmeaning ceremonies of their religion, and were anxious for something better, and that they would hear you gladly. It is therefore a severe disappointment to you to learn that they want nothing to do with you or your religion.

The hindrances to missionary work are numerous and great: not only the prejudices against you as a foreigner whom the natives regard as an enemy, but you are an object of suspicion to the ignorant masses. Fearful stories are told of crimes committed by missionaries against nature and humanity; that they use the eyes and brains of little children for medicine, and many other horrible things. There is no other class so unapproachable as the self-conceited *literati*. They are satisfied with the teachings of Confucius, and with the hoary traditions of their country. They will not listen to the teachings of the missionaries. Like the scribes and Pharisees, they dominate public opinion, and are regarded as the teachers and leaders on all subjects of thought. They shut up the kingdom of heaven against men, for they neither go in themselves, neither suffer them that are entering to go in. (Matthew xxiii. 13.) The hindrances may be summarized briefly: Inveteracy of national and race prejudice; false religions possess the ground; political jealousy of the rulers; social customs; ancestral worship; and the obstinate opposition of all classes against change. Such are some of the difficulties with which the missionary has to contend, in addition to the carnal nature of man which hates God.

The encouragements to hope for ultimate success, if not so numerous as the hindrances, are much more powerful: the promises of God which are full and definite; the success already attained is great; Christian nations control the political and commercial interests of the world; they hold in their vaults the wealth of the world; they command the great armies of the world, and can dictate terms of peace or war to all the heathen nations of the earth; they possess the productive intellect of the world, and are the only nations that are making progress in the arts and sciences. Above all, and beyond all other reasons to hope for the conversion of China, is the inherent divine power of the gospel. Its Author is omnipotent, and his omnipotence is pledged for its ultimate triumph over all its foes; "the heathen are to be given to the Son of God for his inheritance, and the uttermost parts of the earth for his possession." "As I live, saith the Lord, every knee shall bow to me, and every tongue shall confess to God."

It is not strange that a conservative heathen people like the Chinese should dislike to have their religious belief taken from them, and the creed of a stranger substituted in its place; to have all the traditions of a long religious history abolished, and the history and traditions of a comparatively insignificant race (the Jews), of whom they know nothing, made the basis of their new religious faith, and thus required to forsake the faith of their ancestors, whom they venerate with idolatrous superstition. All this we can understand. It is natural. But how men and women who live in a Christian land, and who enjoy the blessings of an advanced Christian civilization, can become the enemies and persecutors of their fellow-countrymen because they have gone to heathen lands to teach the gospel which has created this noble civilization, is not so easily understood.

Among the sharpest trials to which the foreign missionary is exposed are the cruel and unjust criticisms of his own countrymen at home and abroad. The secular press has recently been unusually severe in its animadversions upon the missionaries in China. False accusations have been brought against them. They have been called fools and fanatics, and charged with being the cause of all the troubles in China. This is not the result of ignorance on the part of the critics, for most of them know better, but the spirit of carnal hostility to the gospel.

There are, however, some noble exceptions to the disparaging criticisms of the secular press, even among those who do not proclaim themselves the friends of foreign missions, but who have informed themselves as to the work the foreign missionaries are doing for the heathen, and who have the honesty and the courage to tell the truth.

The recent murder of missionaries in China, and the destruction of mission property, have called forth the sympathies of all good people, and also furnished an occasion for the enemies of righteousness to say many hard and bitter things about missionaries and their work. A better class of people do not live on the face of the earth than the missionaries in China. I know them and I know their work, and I know that what I say as to their character is true in every letter. I had the privilege of living and working in that field for years, and I know whereof I affirm.

The following communication from the Hon. Charles Denby, United States Minister to China, addressed to the Secretary of State, regarding the work of the missionaries in China, is a fair and impartial statement of facts. It was written in March, 1895, and published in all of our leading newspapers, except those unfriendly to the cause of Christian missions. It is an able and ample defense of those devout men and women who are laboring for the good of that benighted and degraded people, "not counting their lives dear unto themselves," but sacrificing everything for the sacred cause they represent. Mr. Denby says:

"The main broad and crucial question to be answered, touching missionary work in China, is: Does it do good? The question may properly be divided into two. Let us look at them separately.

"First. Does missionary work benefit the Chinese? I think that no one can controvert the patent fact that the Chinese are enormously benefited by the labor of the missionaries. Foreign hospitals are a great boon to the sick. China, before the advent of the foreigner, did not know what surgery was. There are more than twenty hospitals in China which are presided over by men of as great ability as can be found elsewhere in the world. Dr. Kerr's hospital is one of the great institutions of its kind in the world. The viceroy, Li Hung Chang, has for years maintained at Tien-Tsin at his own expense a foreign hospital.

"In the matter of education the movement is immense. There are schools and colleges all over China taught by the missionaries. I have been present often at the exhibitions given by these schools. They show progress in a great degree. The educated Chinaman who speaks English becomes a new man. He commences to think. A long time before the war the emperor was studying English, and it is said was fast acquiring the language.

"Nowhere is education more sought than in China. The government is to some extent founded on it. The systems of examination prevailing in the district, the province, and in Peking, are too well known to require comment. The graduates become expectant officials. There is a Chinese imperial college at Peking, the Tung Wen, presided over by our distinguished fellow-citizen, Dr. W. A. P. Martin; also a university conducted by the Methodist mission.

"There are also many foreign orphan asylums in many cities, which take care of thousands of waifs. The missionaries translate into Chinese many scientific and philosophical works. A former missionary, Dr. Edkins, translated a whole series of school readers.

"Reflect that all these benefactions come to the Chinese without much, if any, cost. When charges are made, they are exceedingly small, and are made only when they are necessary to prevent a rush, which in this vast population would overwhelm any institution. There are various anti-opium hospitals, where the victims of this vice are cured. There are industrial schools and workshops.

"This is a very brief and incomplete summary of what missionaries are doing for the Chinese. Protestants and Catholics from nearly every country under the sun are engaged in this work, and in my opinion they do nothing but good. I leave out of this discussion the religious benefits conferred by converting Chinese to Christianity. This, of course, is the one supreme object and purpose of the missionaries, to which all else is subsidiary, but the subject is not to be discussed by a Minister of the United States. There is no established religion in the United States, and the American Buddhist, Mohammedan, Jew, infidel, or any other religionist, would receive at the hands of his country's representatives abroad exactly the same consideration and protection that a Christian would. I can only say that converts to Christianity are numerous. There are supposed to be forty thousand Protestant converts now in China, and at least fifty thousand Catholic converts. There are many native Christian churches. The converts seem to be as devout as people of any other race.

"As far as my knowledge extends, I can and do

say that the missionaries in China are self-sacrificing; that their lives are pure; that they are devoted to their work; that their influence is beneficial to the natives; that the arts and sciences and civilization are greatly spread by their efforts; that many useful Western books are translated by them into Chinese; that they are the leaders in all charitable work, giving largely themselves and personally disbursing the funds with which they are intrusted; that they do make converts, and such converts are mentally benefited by conversion.

"In answer to these statements, which are usually acknowledged to be true, it does not do to say, as if the answer were conclusive, that the *literati* and gentry are usually opposed to missionaries. This antagonism was to have been expected. The missionaries antagonize the worship of ancestors, which is one of the fundamental principles of the Chinese polity. They compel their converts to keep Sunday holy. The Chinese have no Sabbath. They work every day except New-year's day and other holidays. No new religion ever won its way without meeting with serious opposition.

"Under the treaties the missionary has the right to go to China. This right being admitted, no amount of antagonism can prevent its exercise.

"In the second place, let us see whether and how foreign countries are benefited by missionary work done in China.

"Missionaries are the pioneers of trade and

commerce.  Civilization, learning, and instruction breed new wants which commerce supplies.  Look at the electric telegraph now in every province in China but one; look at the steamships which ply along the coast from Hong-Kong to New-Chwang, and on the Yang-tse up the Ichang.  Look at the cities which have sprung up like Shanghai, Tien-Tsin, Hankow—handsome foreign cities, object lessons to the Chinese.  Look at the railroad being now built from the Yellow Sea to the Amoor, of which about two hundred miles are completed.  Will any one say that the fifteen hundred missionaries in China of Protestants, and perhaps more of Catholics, have not contributed to these results?

"Two hundred and fifty years ago the pious Catholic fathers taught astronomy, mathematics, and the languages at Peking.  The interior of China would have been nearly unknown to the outer world had not the missionaries visited it and described it.  Some one may say that commercial agents might have done as much; but they are not allowed to locate in the interior.  The missionary, inspired by holy zeal, goes everywhere, and by degrees foreign commerce and trade follow.  I suppose that whenever an uncivilized or semi-civilized country becomes civilized, its trade and dealings with Western nations increase.  Humanity has not devised any better, or even as good, engine or means for civilizing savage peoples as proselytism to Christianity.  The history of the world attests this fact.

"In the interests, therefore, of civilization, missionaries ought not only to be tolerated, but ought to receive protection to which they are entitled from officials and encouragement from other classes of people.

"It is too early now to consider what effect the existing war may have on the interests of missions. It is quite probable, however, that the spirit of progress developed by it will make mission work more important and influential than it has ever been."

Bishop Hendrix says of Colonel Denby, whom he met in Peking during his recent visit to China:

"Colonel Charles Denby, American Minister to China, is the dean of the diplomatic corps in Peking, having already served his country there for the past ten years. The exceptional honor shown him of being continued at his important post during the political changes at home is due to his marked fitness for his present position. Eminent as a lawyer in this country, his legal learning has been of great service to the Chinese empire no less than to his own countrymen. His clear statement to the Secretary of State of the value and progress of Christian missions in China has attracted wide attention. He has no sympathy with the globe-trotters or naval officers whose knowledge of China is confined to a few treaty ports, and who have never looked into the work being done by missionaries, and yet who presume to pronounce unfavorable and unjust judgment on what they know nothing about. Having the confidence of the Tsung Li Yamen, the foreign office of China, as no other ambassador has, in view of his valued counsels during the late war and by virtue of his long official residence in Peking, Colonel Denby is in position to form a correct judgment, if anyone can do so. Much weight should therefore be given to the language of his dispatch to his government near the close of the war, when he said: 'It is quite probable that the spirit of progress developed by the war will make mission work more important and influential than ever.'"

LI HUNG CHANG.

# CONCLUSION.

## The Present Condition of China.

I HAVE not the information necessary to a discussion of the present political condition of China. Even men well informed in regard to the East generally, and for many years resident in China, seem unable to comprehend the situation; not only because it is difficult to ascertain the facts involved in the question, but also because of the complications produced by the results of the recent war between China and Japan. This phase of Chinese politics must be left to the developments of time and the skill of diplomacy. The Christian world will naturally contemplate with great concern the probable effects of the war upon the success of missions in China. It is too early to forecast, with any degree of certainty, what the results will be. In lieu of any opinion of my own on the subject, I quote the last two paragraphs of an article by Bishop Hendrix, in the May-June (1896) number of the Southern *Methodist Review*. The bishop enjoyed exceptional opportunities for gathering information in regard to the affairs of China during his recent visit, being admitted to interviews with the highest dignitaries of the empire, notably with Li Hung Chang, the greatest statesman in Asia; and also with the representatives of foreign countries resident at Peking. The bishop is hopeful. The message sent through him from Li Hung Chang ought to thrill the heart of Christendom. Will the Churches of America heed this "Macedonian cry?" The bishop says:

"The late war has done more to open the way for the salvation of China than any event in her hoary history. Her old leaders recognize their helplessness, and are seeking counsel. Reform clubs are being formed by her ablest scholars, who are asking papers from Christian missionaries and statesmen as to what reforms China most needs, and the best way of bringing them about. The able papers on education which were prepared for the Japanese government by Christian scholars in America and Europe are now being translated into Chinese for the use of the newly awakened among the sleeping masses of the Chinese empire. The payment of a great war indemnity is making necessary the development of the hidden resources of the country. Grave mounds are no longer a protection to the plains which are required for the roadbed of great trunk lines, or to hillsides which hide the mineral wealth of the land. Other massacres may yet occur, for the evil spirit will rend and tear the victim ere he consents to be exorcised; but China, stunned by a great blow, is not indifferent to the good Samaritan who waits by her bleeding form to pour in oil and wine. A Christian missionary has been asked to become foreign adviser to the Chinese government. Chinese officials of highest rank now ask the once despised missionary and foreigner what can be done for their humiliated country. The greatest Chinaman of his century, and the foremost statesman of Asia, Li Hung Chang, after building hospitals where foreign medical and surgical skill could be had to relieve the sufferings of his countrymen, and establishing colleges where foreign science could be taught the promising youth of China, chosen from the various mission schools where they had received their earlier training, and expressing his profound sense of obligation on the part of his country for the great service done by the schools and hospitals established by Christian missionaries, apologizes to the Christian world for the atrocities of his ignorant and brutal fellow-countrymen by sending this message: '*Say to the American people for me, to send over more men for the schools and the hospitals, and I hope to be in position both to aid them and protect them.*'

"This is China's one articulate message to the Christian nations which see her unstanched wounds, received in a war everywhere disastrous by land and sea. Nothing short of such humiliation could have called out such an acknowledgment of helplessness and of need. 'Lo, these shall come from far; and lo, these from the north and from the west; and these from the land of Sinim.'"

www.ingramcontent.com/pod-product-compliance
Lightning Source LLC
Chambersburg PA
CBHW022335230426
**43664CB00040B/1110**